PRAISE FOR

Joie Goodkin AND You Can Do It!

"I wish everyone could meet Joie as I did and have 3 hours of
1:1 inspiring conversation over dinner. But thankfully,
now her book can deliver her message of confidence
and trailblazing into the hands of so many!
You will be as captivated by her words of wisdom as I was.
I promise you will walk away from reading this book
more inspired and confident in business."

NANCY GALLAS SHAMBERG
Managing Partner, TracyLocke Chicago

"With wisdom and wit, Joie Goodkin is a role model
for all generations of women. Her stories of courage, intuition,
grace and grit will inspire and motivate anyone to burst
through barriers and blaze their own path."

DEBORAH KOCH
Executive Director, American Red Cross Greater Miami & The Keys

"The life lessons Joie Goodkin shares in this compelling book
will inspire readers to reach for the gold in their own careers
and personal lives and passionately embrace the rewards
of "giving back" to their communities. Joie Goodkin has rallied
thousands to stand on a beach for charity while creating a thriving
business and living a full family life—she candidly and passionately
shares how others can accomplish much for others while
enjoying success at home and in their careers."

JON B. DEVRIES. AICP
Co-Author, Planning Chicago, Routledge,
and VP, Land Economics Foundation, LAI, Founding Director,
Marshall Bennett Institute of Real Estate, Roosevelt University, Chicago

You Can Do It!

For Debbie, Sarah,
Valarie, Sherrie, Andria,
Jessica, Zach and Alex

Contents

INTRODUCTION: You Ought to Write a Book!.............. xi

CHAPTER ONE: Profit Knows No Sex 1

CHAPTER TWO: Perseverance Pays Off 19

CHAPTER THREE: Trust Your Intuition..................... 39

CHAPTER FOUR: All Anybody Buys are Benefits............ 57

CHAPTER FIVE: Always Fill a Need........................ 69

CHAPTER SIX: Put Yourself in Another's Shoes 87

CHAPTER SEVEN: Create Win-Win Situations................ 101

CHAPTER EIGHT: Pick Smart People and
Let Them Do Their Jobs..................... 115

CHAPTER NINE: Taking the Courageous Step............... 129

CHAPTER TEN: Be Open to an Unexpected Awakening....... 139

ABOUT THE AUTHOR 163

ACKNOWLEDGMENTS 165

You Ought to Write a Book!

*"If you think you can, or you think you can't,
you're right."*

— HENRY FORD

This book has its origins in a chance encounter from a couple of years ago when my husband was having an operation in a San Francisco-area hospital. I had gone back to our hotel for dinner, and in the restaurant line in front of me was a young woman who appeared to be alone. When she told the hostess "table for one," I spoke up: "Excuse me, would you like some company for dinner? I'm really very nice and if you don't think so, you can just get up and leave. But maybe we'll enjoy each other and have a nice meal together."

She gave me one of the most quizzical looks, but I just smiled back and, more or less, charmed my way into getting a table together. Her name was Nancy and she was a retail marketing manager in town on business. It must have been some kind of fate that the two of us connected!

Over our meal, I told her some stories about when I was a business creator and owner and before we knew it, we had been sitting at that table for three hours.

Nancy related to a lot of my company building and marketing strategies, and particularly to a lot of my thoughts about how a woman can successfully project herself in male-dominated situations by using skills and abilities to present yourself as an incredible person.

Before we parted, she told me "you're inspiring me so much, you just have to write a book."

"Oh Nancy, people have been telling me for years that I should write a book, but I don't know what I'd say, or what I'd write about, or who'd want to read it."

"I'd want to read it," she assured. "If it wasn't for trailblazing women like you, I wouldn't be where I am."

She and I stayed in touch, became friends on Facebook and sent occasional emails. She once told me that she did this and did that, mostly because, she said, "You gave me the confidence that I could do it."

In the intervening time since meeting Nancy, I thought a lot about our conversation, especially after other women began telling me the same thing: "You ought to write a book!" So many women were telling me how my example and my stories had somehow helped them in their careers.

As I reflect back on my own path, I was a trailblazer in business, no doubt, as evidenced by the fact that I was often the only woman sitting on the board of either a bank or some other institution, or the only woman participating in a business meeting or non-profit group's committee. I was even one of the first women ever invited to break the gender barrier in Rotary International.

A lot of working women in Broward County, Florida were in real estate during the 1970s, but my situation was different because I had started my own series of businesses. As the men sort of forgot I was a woman, they respected my opinions more. They admired my problem solving skills. There was a glass ceiling, for sure, but I was never aware of it or felt hindered by it.

My attitude was always "who says I can't do that?" I have always felt that other people's opinions do not have to limit any of us, we only limit ourselves. Their opinions are not reality.

I was a novelty without realizing it, but I was always careful to make an impression that wouldn't hurt other women who were trying to enter the business world. These other women were looking at me like a bellwether.

In those days, some restaurants would not even let women in who wore pant suits; that's how nuts traditional social rules were at times. In response, I always projected the best image so everyone would take me seriously. I also respected divergent views and my secret was to try and find common threads between us. That is the best technique for conflict resolution. If we can agree on a thread, maybe we can create a spool.

This book is for women who want to have a bigger career, or a different career, but it can be helpful to anyone really. It's about building confidence to take risks and assert goals. A thirty-something-businesswoman named Maria commented to me: "It's about learning to feel powerful enough to claim what we want. Women don't always feel worthy. We are still programmed to hold back, not to aggressively pursue what we want."

My granddaughter, Sarah, inspired me too, by what she wanted to see in this book. These are some of her thoughts: "What is relevant, in a timeless way, is learning that we need to feel confidence. Confidence is a huge issue. Feeling confident and knowing how to affect that personal connection in order to achieve goals; treating people with respect and learning to see situations from the other person's point of view; standing your ground and believing that what you want is worth fighting for; and being able to push forward when necessary because women are not usually trained or raised to be that way. It's also okay to make yourself heard, or you won't be heard. This applies to a lot of areas of life. All of this is human centered and all of us could benefit from developing our abilities to be confident, be forward and be heard."

When my daughter Debbie was a little kid still learning to put on shoes and socks, she would become annoyed as her little sock would somehow get stuck and not make it over her heel to pull all the way up. Rather than fix it for her, I created a little song, "You Can Do It," and we would sing the lyrics "you can do it" over and over. Soon she would be pulling that sock on and singing, turning a frustrating experience into a fun one. The lesson from her little socks still applies and now serves decades later as this book's title.

What is it that pushes us to succeed or to just go for it? I think it is a knowing that there is a force within us that guides and encourages us. It might manifest as chutzpah, moxie, or nerve, or just as a driving need to accomplish something.

This book can inspire anyone, and it includes some things that are valuable to starting a business and increasing your sales, building your business through choosing the right employees, not taking yourself too seriously, and realizing that rejection of your ideas is not to be taken personally.

Have confidence in your own abilities to make your life happen as you know it can be! Think that you can do it and you are halfway there! I hope this book deeply impacts you as you relate my stories directly to helping give direction to your ideas and transform your life! Even if you don't ever create a business or switch from your current job, this book is about cultivating confidence.

Confidence is revealed by that extra zing in your step, that glow on your face and that knowingness in your smile. It makes you go for it! Like Henry Ford said, "If you think you can or you think you can't, you're right."

This book is meant to show you that YES, You Can Do It!

CHAPTER ONE

Profit Knows No Sex

JOIE-ISM #1

Assert Your Power. Ever go into a meeting where
the guy behind the desk points to a chair you are supposed
to sit in? My advice is to smile and find another place to sit.
It's a subtle way of shifting the power in the room and may even
be enough for you to give notice about your assertiveness.
This is particularly true if you are a woman.

In April 1945, as a three-year-old, I was held high in my father's arms on a New York City street, watching the funeral procession of President Franklin Roosevelt. People stood at least ten rows deep, their only sounds being weeps of grief. A defining moment in my life came some years after, at the age of eleven, when I had the honor of introducing Eleanor Roosevelt, the widow of President Roosevelt, to a large audience packed into my elementary school auditorium. It's a bit of a blur as to how it happened that I was chosen to introduce her, but I believe the school student council president was supposed to do it, but became sick. By default, the honor fell to me as the sixth-grade representative to the student council.

Eleanor Roosevelt towered over me, not only with her physical appearance—tall and stout—but with her radiance and wisdom too. That day she was wearing a plum-colored simple dress with a matching belt and buckle made of the same fabric, and I remember thinking: *she isn't very fashionable.*

I recall too that though this was my first time speaking in front of an audience, I felt calm and empowered. She stood regally, radiating a bright wisdom and depth of spirit. She smiled at me and touched my left shoulder as she told me something about my future being whatever I wanted it to be, if I worked hard, was determined to succeed, and persevered to create my dreams, whatever they may be. All this was conveyed in less than a minute, yet it was so enriching that I credit it with a lifelong belief, that yes, if any one of us puts our minds to something, we can turn an idea into a reality.

She still remains one of my special heroines just by having simply stood there smiling, being herself, radiating a strength and solidness. Her presence was enough for me, though the words she spoke added extra weight to her total countenance.

In stark contrast, that same year my family visited California, and as a special treat we were taken to the Warner Bros. Studio lot to see the filming of "Calamity Jane" starring Doris Day. I stood there fascinated by the façade of the stage set and the realization that it was all an elaborate make-believe. Nothing was true or solid. And the cast and crew repeated a short scene in a barroom at least twelve times—it got boring to watch, and the numerous retakes all seemed hardly worthy of so many people giving it so much effort and attention. But I was polite and continued to watch. When they finally took a break, Doris Day came over to our group and introduced herself to us individually. I told her my name and she smiled and said, "Would you like my autograph?"

I was perplexed. "What do I do with an autograph?" I truly had no idea why her signature would be valuable to me.

She seemed to have left in a huff, and the other people who were acting self-important puffed up their chests and held their heads high as they went back to shooting.

The experience left me with the feeling that make-believe stuff might be entertaining, but it wasn't special to me. I much preferred real depth instead of flounce. I still am not impressed with celebrities just for the sake of celebrity, and perhaps this Calamity Jane experience is at the root of that feeling.

I admire strength of purpose, wisdom, deep caring for others, and knowingness. The twinkle and depth I saw in Eleanor Roosevelt's eyes became a model for me and a constant source of inspiration for how I lived my life. Doris Day ultimately inspired me too, as she was a great activist for animal rights. My dog, Yogi, was even given a seat, treats and his own bowl in the bar at her hotel in Carmel.

Becoming Your Authentic Self

It has been valuable for me to realize how much courage it takes to grow up and be my authentic self. I was never supposed to have a business. I was programmed to grow up to become a teacher, or a nurse, or a secretary, and find a man to marry who was going to make enough money for me to have a good life. We would want two kids, and a big mortgage, which would be better than a small mortgage, and if I had a low golf handicap, I had it made. None of those options particularly appealed to me, even from an early age.

That wasn't who I was or what I wanted to be. You too can recognize that you can follow blindly what you think you're supposed to be doing, or you can say to yourself, "Is this what I really want to do? Is this who I really want to become?"

When I saw the movie, *The Help,* which was set in 1962 in the Deep South, I realized it was the year I got married at age 21. I watched that movie and felt a tremendous sense of despair that I didn't travel there and try to help make a difference in the justice and civil rights causes. The white women in the South in that movie were my contemporaries, treating their help nicely, because that's what was expected of them. But by the time the movie is over, I realized how they were so narrow-minded and bigoted that they didn't see the hired help as human beings, much less as friends.

I should have gotten myself down there and gotten involved. Two of my friends who were lawyers actually went and worked with the three men who died in the *Mississippi Burning* story. My friends came back completely different than when they left. You may think you know what's going on in the world, but when you experience it firsthand it will have a much greater impact. A lot of us were so sheltered then that we didn't really know the extent of the injustices.

Newly married and having just started a teaching job, I wondered when would there be time to run to Mississippi? I felt like there was a part of me that was unfulfilled because I cared so much, yet I couldn't quite bridge that gap at the time. As I got older, I was able to say to myself *hey, wait a minute lady, this is what you really want to do and you still don't do it? Just do it!*

Advocating for Job Gender Equality

City magazines were popping up all over the country in the 1970s, creating many events and publishing conventions for me to attend and participate in. At one such event, I met Gloria Steinem, publisher of *Ms. Magazine*, a bright, warm lady with a lot of charm. She beamed at me and said she would like to write a feature on me and my magazine, *Broward Life*.

It was an easy decision for me to turn her down. "Gloria, I love men! Your magazine appears to bash them and position women as being somehow better. That doesn't work for me. I think the thrust of what is written should respect that both women and men have talent, and both should have equal opportunity to pursue careers, be promoted, and advance due to their skills and not their gender."

She seemed surprised by my answer, but hopefully understood my point. The last place I would want to appear would be in a publication that touted women at the expense of men. *I never tried to act like a man and I didn't disparage them.*

When it came to much of what was known back then as women's liberation, I associated that movement with loud women shouting about stuff that made me uncomfortable. I never understood why singling out women or men made any sense when it came to choosing the best person for the job, or in judging job performance.

Today, I think I would understand their frustrations better. Decades have passed since I interacted with Gloria Steinem, and while progress certainly has been made, there is still a wide rift between equal pay and equal respect between the sexes. You would need to be an ostrich with your head in the sand not to believe the plethora of sexual harassment lawsuits prove there is a problem.

Whenever there is a closing off of talent or ideas due to gender, I believe that the entire organization suffers. Without a real change in how young people are educated about this and so many other key social justice issues of our time, it would seem we are doomed to futility like Sisyphus and to keep repeating our actions that have turned out to be mistakes. Mistakes because our society as a whole does not fully benefit from the talent pool and wisdom of so many women. Mutual respect for individuals, regardless of gender or other identifying labels, is what strengthens us all.

The men who were my biggest supporters and advocates always were touting my accomplishments and recommending me for some committee or board. I never thought of myself as anyone special because of my gender. Others had different ideas, as I was often asked "What's it like to be a woman publisher?" I admonished a reporter once who asked me that, "Well, according to your standards I would make a great husband for someone!"

On one occasion I found myself sitting at lunch at a round table for eight, with seven of my loyal male supporters in the Tower Club, atop a bank building in Fort Lauderdale. The vast majority of members in this tony business club were male. During the course of this lunch the subject of women's liberation came up in an oblique way.

"You're not one of those women's libbers!" remarked one of my advocates.

"I do believe in equal pay for equal work."

As mouths slackened and eyes focused on me, I elaborated. "If you had a great candidate for a job, or had someone in your organization doing an outstanding job, would you really think it was a good idea to base your opinion primarily on whether they were male or female? What real difference is there if the job gets done well by the best person you have to do it?"

Their collective reaction was to focus on the food on their plates, their eyes averted, or else they looked just about anywhere but in my direction. It was as if I had dropped a dead mouse in the middle of the table. I tried to change the subject, but it was an awkward moment because these guys were frozen with quizzical expressions on their faces and obvious degrees of discomfort.

Fearless me had no idea they would react that way, as I had no love for the big-hatted Bella Abzug and others who I found to be a noisy distraction from the central issue of fairness in paying people equally for the same work, irrespective of their gender.

Being a Successful Woman in Business

Every month I wrote a column titled "Up Front" for my *Broward Life Magazine*. In a July 1978 issue, which featured profiles of women who were "successful members of this community who also happen to be female," I addressed how I viewed the role of women in business:

> Many people assume that they know what I think about women. Since I'm a woman in business they figure I must be strongly interested in women's liberation, for example, or related causes and organizations. In the current socio-political context that has come to define 'women's liberation,' however, these assumptions are wrong.
>
> I am in favor of equal pay for equal work, of course, but in many ways today I find the women's lib movement confused, self-righteous and embarrassingly atavistic. So, when someone perceives me, a businesswoman, as necessarily a crusader, I categorize that as ignorant of the roles modern woman has come to assume in this society.
>
> In the real world all are equal before the bottom line. Profit and loss know no sex. Neither does

accomplishment. To some people it seems very
important that I am a woman publisher. To me
it's more important that I am a publisher who just
happens to be a woman. Identity is not a composite
of genetic characteristics alone; it is a composite of
what one has done as well.

To illustrate the misconceptions many people held about women
in business in those days, there was a morning when my wonderful
white Cadillac wouldn't start. I called AAA to come and start the car.
This man came out, a little skinny guy, and he was looking around at
the back of the car and then under the hood. I was standing there in
a business suit and a nice silk blouse, wearing high heels, and holding
a briefcase. He looked at my car and my car phone, then looked at me
so perplexed and asked, "Whose secretary are you?"

In those days a woman executive, or a woman in business, was
not typically seen. The man assumed if I was dressed for business,
I must have been someone's secretary, which was kind of amusing
to me at the time because I had two secretaries of my own.

In May 1977, I was approached by some of my good friends
in Broward County, Florida, with whom I served on civic boards
and committees, about attending a Rotary meeting and joining
Rotary International. One man headed up the telephone company
and another was in charge of the power company. My friend from
the telephone company, Ed, really pushed hard for me to join
Rotary, so I finally said yes. Then Ed was totally mortified when he
inquired about my attendance, because it turned out that Rotary
had a national policy of not accepting women as members.

Even though you could do all kinds of wonderful things in the
community as a woman, and you could be the publisher of a local
magazine, you couldn't be a member of their civic association
and be involved in their projects to benefit the community. This
really embarrassed Ed and he hemmed and hawed and finally
proposed a compromise: We could send a male emissary from
Broward Life Magazine. I chose my advertising manager at the
time, a charming glad-handing man, and he went in my place.

His function was to sell more ads while socializing with all of these businessmen.

The Rotary Club members had an annual dinner in which their significant other or spouse could also attend as a guest. I got to attend this Rotary dinner as the guest of my own advertising manager. This was so typical of how women were treated at the time that I didn't give it a whole lot of thought. But when I got to the dinner and sat down, they handed everyone a program to tell about the event in it and they had listed my advertising manager as publisher of *Broward Life Magazine*. That certainly got me riled up.

I didn't mind paying the Rotary dues for one of my employees to attend their meetings, but now they've got this employee recognized as having my job! I thought, *I don't think so!* To me that was just a horrible presumption. So I refused to pay any more Rotary dues and wouldn't allow my employee to attend any more of their meetings or events.

Ed and a few others felt beyond mortified by what happened and tried to solicit Rotary to change their point of view about women as members. They wrote to Rotary's headquarters in Washington, D.C. proposing that the rules be changed to accept women. About a year passed and nothing happened. But finally one day I got a call from Ed: "They've written to me that they're considering taking women and you would be the first one they would ask."

Some official at Rotary International did invite me to join their organization, but the invitation came just as I was getting ready to sell the magazine. I no longer had any real reason to want to become a member of Rotary, so I declined nicely, thank you, but no thank you. In retrospect, it's always been interesting to me that I was one of the trailblazers for getting women invited into Rotary and maybe I should have joined just to make my trailblazing official.

Making the Most of "Tokenism"

A pattern seemed to emerge for me showing the less I knew about a subject, the more likely I would be asked to serve as the only woman on a board that featured it. For example, when I was elected President of the United Way of Broward County, Florida in 1985, I recall thinking I had been the only woman, or possibly one of few women on that board. Though I never planned to serve on these various boards, it seemed a natural outgrowth of all of my volunteerism and activism in the community. I was respected for my contributions, which may have started out to be just little more than a token gesture for my gender; but ultimately my value was recognized. I was delighted to be asked to serve on the First Federal of Broward Advisory Board, as this was a local savings and loan, and it paid a whopping $1,200 monthly fee (a hefty sum in those days) for attending a meeting that lasted between two and three hours. This was in the early 1980s, and my husband Lew and I had just returned from a trip to Hong Kong, where I did what most tourists did back then: bought custom-made clothing—several business suits from the typical pinstripe navy to dark grey gabardine. I was asked to join this board soon after we returned home.

"Oh, goody! I can wear my new suits," was my actual response.

The gentleman, Philip N. Cheney, who invited me to join, was president of the bank and one of my career "rabbis" in Florida. He often was instrumental in appointing me to various positions in both the local and state business scene. I went on to serve on this board for several years until it merged with new owners, Glendale Federal Savings and Loan out of California. I was then asked to stay on this new Florida Board for Glendale Federal, and in both cases, was the only woman.

Chuckling "Lady and Gentlemen" was how they would start meetings. Ridiculously enough, they gave me a tie for Christmas during my first year on the Glendale Federal Board. It was adorned with the logo of the bank. I handed it off to Tony, my first press operator, and cautioned him, "Don't wear it near the press or you could have a rollup!" A rollup meant that the tie would find itself wrapped around the rollers or other press parts. Tony possibly wore it to one of our elaborate Christmas parties.

I always wondered why banks paid their tellers so little as they were the people meeting the customers. It seemed to me a bank that paid more for tellers would attract greater customer-oriented employees. They called this "bottoms up marketing" in those days, but the bank likely never did take my advice, however I did manage to bring them some great loan customers, and took my role very seriously as a representative of their organization.

The first time I met the chairman of Glendale Federal was when their top brass came from California and we all took a yacht up and down the Intracoastal Waterway. "Hi," I said, moving towards him. "I'm the only *redhead* on the board."

At first he was taken aback, but it was my way of announcing that yes, I was their token something—in my case, a token woman. I suppose if I had also been Black or Latino and a woman, who knows how much more valuable I could have been perceived to be. At least there was some awareness of diversity in those days.

It was amusing to me over time that I was the one asked to present difficult ideas to this chairman, as I was one of the few people on the board not beholden to the bank in any way. I was their special emissary to tell him stuff that none of the others wanted to.

What really surprised me among all of my appointments was being asked by then Governor Martinez to serve on the State Transportation Board. I had been appointed to positions by three different Florida governors, and recall telling the state senator who approached me about the transportation offer, "If I say yes, does it mean I agree with Martinez?" "Well, yes," the senator answered, but nobody really made much of that, and there I was serving on another board that I knew zilch about.

Back east we called them thruways, and in California, they are freeways, but to me they were all big roads to be avoided because I didn't like to drive. I would find myself lost and exiting in the wrong places more often than I cared to count. However, when I would arrive for a meeting or to take a client to lunch with a driver, in either a limo or a town car instead of driving myself, I always got a significant contract out of it. Perception in those days was all part of my presentation to impress on a client how important they were to the success of either my magazine or my printing and graphics company.

A big topic of discussion for the Transportation Board I served on was the upcoming long-term repair of Interstate 95, which traversed the entire length of the state. The work was expected to take years. They were calling it the I-95 Reconstruction. They yacked and jawed for hours about this. During one board meeting, I spoke up (which was rare, as I really usually didn't have a clue about what they were discussing) and observed, "Calling it I-95 Reconstruction sounds like years of inconvenience. If you call it repairs it sounds like a fix, but not that permanent. So why not call it the I-95 Expansion, that way it appears to offer more when it is complete?"

Everyone really liked that idea and so it was named the I-95 Expansion Project! My company designed the banners and logos for the signage of that huge project and when it came time to bid on the state printing for that job, we actually won. It was a huge printing contract, but unfortunately I came to learn that the state was almost in the "net never" category, meaning they took forever to pay their bills. As a result, I never bid on another state job.

I had a system for estimating the work for these very large jobs. If we figured the "per piece" cost and rounded it down to .09 cents, we didn't always get the job. But if we really wanted the job, we could practically be guaranteed to get it if we rounded it down to .04 cents. Depending on the likelihood of reorders, we would do this, and it never seemed to fail. Once you had the printing plates, it was simple to get all the reruns.

My secret weapon for estimating was to tell the estimator, "Use the rule of 4 or 7 or whatever we think will be a low enough per piece price to beat out the competition." The difference in the profitability of the job was always negligible and we made it up in having many big volume jobs that would generate repeat business.

Still another barrier I breeched in the business world was in the realm of planning civic improvements. The Broward Workshop was formed as the direct result of several of us community leaders meeting privately in the back room of a lumber company owned by one of Broward's most influential businessmen. When I was first invited to attend these backroom meetings, I was confused as to why I was included; but by that time, I guess it made sense because I was on bank boards, civic boards and had published a locally respected magazine.

There were about seven men and me. We discussed things needing improvement in the county, and were given assignments as to who would approach whom to get things done. We were a truly civic-minded endeavor and it has evolved today to include leaders from Broward's top 100 businesses. This growth took decades, but it was started back in the late 1970s and early 1980s in that backroom.

A Special Award, a Not-So Special Dress, and Being Lied To

When I received the Silver Medallion Award at the 33rd Annual Brotherhood Awards Dinner of the National Conference of Christians and Jews for their 50th Anniversary in Florida, it was a memorable event and a big deal for me. The venue was in a Miami ballroom before 1,400 people with then CBS News anchor and *60 Minutes* correspondent Diane Sawyer presenting the awards.

I was the first female recipient of this honor, though I shared that distinction with another winner that year, Sister Mercy, who headed Holy Cross Hospital Foundation.

Upon hearing that I was selected as a recipient, I thought I should "wear something dignified" and envisioned myself in a long dress with a halter type top that would have a high neck; either black or perhaps grey cashmere, and very sophisticated. When I went shopping for a long dress, everything looked too flouncy and totally wrong for the occasion.

We lived near the Galleria Mall in Fort Lauderdale, so I scoured the shops there for something more appropriate. I ventured into a women's clothing store called Lilly Rubin and saw a long black and silver gown that was slim, with a low-cut top and spaghetti straps holding it up. It had tons of silver bugle beads, and a silver beaded belt. I liked how I looked in it, but admitted to myself and my husband that it wasn't exactly what I thought I would wind up with.

It was the most expensive dress I had ever bought, but the store manager made a huge point of telling me that it was the only dress like it in South Florida, and it would be a smashing success to wear to receive an award. When I showed up at the event, one of the first people I saw was one of the men who had nominated me for the award. He ran to grab a jacket for me to throw on over my new dress. He was clucking like a mother hen, but I did decline the jacket!

Once on the podium to receive the award, I made some remarks and thanked the appropriate people, and then commented, "I wore this particular dress so no one would confuse me with Sister Mercy!"

That got a huge laugh from the crowd. On a more serious note, I told them about the holocaust survivor who tailored the gown for me, and how much it meant to her that I was wearing it to receive an award from an organization that honored brotherhood and welcomed all faiths and traditions as equals.

An unusual coda to this story was several weeks later I was eating lunch at Neiman Marcus in that same mall, and noticed the same dress on a mannequin offered for half the price I had paid at Lilly Rubin, and it was the same size as mine. I was shocked, as the store manager was very clear that mine was the only one of that design in South Florida.

I ran to the Lilly Rubin store and told the manager, but she just shrugged . . . "I didn't expect Neiman's to have it, *blah blah*." Well, in those days it was fair to call me a tough cookie, but I was appalled that she had not kept her word. As you will see in many stories in this book, I believe that you, your character, and who you are as a person are only as strong as your ability to keep your word.

This store manager just blew me off and I found that to be totally unacceptable! I wrote a letter to the chairman of the

Lilly Rubin company and shared what happened without ever mentioning the price of the dress. Shortly thereafter, I received a letter from him asking me if I would like to return the dress for full credit. YES! It gave me a great deal of pleasure to drop it on that store manager's desk, like it was a limp, although sparkly, rat! I handed her the letter and she credited my account without uttering so much as a word—but I did hear a small groan.

That was the same year that Donna Karan showed her first collection and I was able to buy several pieces that I kept for two decades, using those Lilly Rubin funds.

Ultimately this experience had a great outcome, but I never shopped at Lilly Rubin again. My experience of not being told the truth was the reason I was motivated to seek retribution. Had she said that it was not the only one that existed in South Florida, that special dress might still be in my closet.

Scaling the Walls of Madison Avenue While Your Nails Are Still Wet

There were always opportunities to meet with people, exchange business cards and make small talk with prospective clients and advertisers when you showed up at a convention. My husband, Lew, would attend many real estate related conferences and conventions, and often he was a keynote speaker. He has a gift for making complex issues and ideas funny and clever. Responses to his speeches always included a lot of laughter. At many of these conventions that I attended as a spouse there was a "spouse program" (yawn), but I preferred to attend parts of the convention that were designed for the attendees. Once in a while they would offer to take us spouses on a bus to a museum. That sort of treatment was the norm.

It seems really quaint now, but that is how things were in those days. Men still thought the spouses needed their own separate program, and it had to be something of particular interest to them. I was asked to speak at some of these conventions, but not to the attendees, who were always predominantly male. By being allowed to speak to their spouses though, it got me into a few conventions, but then came the question, what to talk about with a room full of just women? This gave me the idea to find other conventions to attend by offering to speak to the spouses.

Women in the early days of my career were either housewives, teachers, nurses or secretaries. It seemed that they would of course know more than I would about those careers, so I found myself acting as a cheerleader to offer them more of a perspective on what else they might do in addition to their everyday activities, if they wanted to find more fulfillment.

Most of my presentations for spouses at these conventions did relate to cooking and presenting food beautifully, but I also did some talks on fashion, color combinations, art and the joy of just grabbing some paints or colored pencils and doing a design as it happened to flow from your brush or pencil to the paper. The underlying theme was to use whatever appealed to each person to actively create something. In that act of creating, they discovered more about what they liked and enjoyed. I also would always add a scarf to tie an outfit together, but just changing the style of earrings or being a little bit differently dressed than their usual attire could inspire them to step a little bolder and enjoy themselves a bit more. I also would encourage my listeners to go after a job that would have been deemed unlikely at the time. "You have nothing to lose by trying something new," I advised.

Just creating and sharing thoughts on paper was something anyone could do too. They could have a book of short stories, a novel, or recipe cards put in a special creatively done box to be a gift; how special that would be. All of these kinds of topics and more became part of my convention repertoire of "Scaling the Walls of Madison Avenue While Your Nails are Still Wet!"

My real purpose in being at these conventions was to sell more ads for *Broward Life Magazine*. This visual for me—getting appointments with ad agency guys, particularly for national advertising from New York City agencies—prompted and explained the title of my presentation to the spouses. Going after these guys to sell an ad! That was me! Local agencies did have women, and really smart and creative ones, but my recollection is that in those days most of the deciders were guys. Getting to them in creative ways, and sharing those thoughts with their spouses, helped me open many doors, and also helped me walk through them.

When Someone Doesn't Represent Their Company Well

Florida was a big printing mecca in the late 1970s and early to mid-80s, and hosted a trade show every year in Miami. Printers, photographers, and buyers of all kinds of equipment related to the trade would gather to view new products, greet old friends, and in the hopes of the vendors, buy something. I happily attended for several years and became friendly with many of the vendors.

My cousin, Mort Goodkin, would be there every year, as he manufactured equipment in those days and was known at the time for the "Goodkin lucy," an enlarging machine he had invented. He provided one to our prepress department at JMG. He introduced me around and the two of us would walk about and meet a lot of fellow printing guys.

One year I went to the conference specifically because I wanted to buy a cutting machine, a folder and my favorite, a Heidelberg press. Bouncing over to their booth I asked about some of this equipment. "Bring ya husband around" was the drawling answer from their salesman.

"Uh, he's not in the printing business."

The guy turned away from me to look for any possible other prospect he could interact with. I went off to find Cousin Morty so he could tell this guy that, yes, I was in the printing business. But he didn't seem likable enough to me to even want Morty to convince him that I was worth talking to, even if I was just a woman.

So Morty and I went back and waited to deal with someone else, and soon I had the attention of another guy working the booth. I asked a lot of questions, as that was my main way of learning about stuff that I knew nothing about. After I understood the merits of this cutter over that one, I considered choosing a folder, and after that talked about getting a Heidelberg press. Once the order was written up, the first guy looking stunned tried to smile at me. Not only had he lost the commission, mine turned out to be one of their bigger sales of that event.

I felt some sort of trailblazing obligation to write to the U.S. president of Heidelberg sales and inform him of how I was treated at the Miami Printing Trade Show. After all, not every woman interested in their products would have a cousin there that could pave the way.

He actually called me and we shared a mutually enjoyable conversation. I told him how much our guys loved their new equipment and what big fans we were of Heidelberg. I mentioned that we had made up a cheer, *Give me an H . . . Give me an E . . .* etc. The following year, surprise! I received from Heidelberg a gift of airfare and two tickets to the major printing show in Chicago. I happily attended and met more of their guys who could not have been more gracious.

If you find yourself dealing with someone who doesn't represent their company well, the person at the top will appreciate knowing of your experience. The key is to be professional, gracious and come from a place of caring and wanting to right a wrong. I think you will get a positive response that way. Today, letter writing is rare so it will likely get attention. If no one lets those executives know, they may remain oblivious to the problem.

Cultivating Confidence Is a Great Gift

I've been asked many times, what do you think is the secret to your success? I truly believe it is because I was always underestimated.

Consider the event I organized for the 60,000 people on the beach for United Way described later in this book. People told me you'll never be able to do that. "Yes, I will," was my confident response. We wanted 40,000 people to participate and we got 60,000, exceeding everyone's expectations.

Having confidence in yourself and being able to effectively express that is one of the greatest gifts you can have. If you learn something in this book from my experiences that can give you confidence, that would be a phenomenal outcome and make this book all the more worthwhile. I've noticed in my life that when I am around people who seem to be very shy, they get used to being more assertive because they see how I can be and what I can do. If you think you can't accomplish what you want, or think you're too shy to ask for it, then think about what's the worst that can happen if people don't respond favorably to you? It has nothing to do with you—it's all about the other person. It just takes a little courage to push yourself much further than you thought you could go.

ᒍOIE-ISM #2

Act serious, and treat your goals seriously,
but never take yourself too seriously.
It's important to learn when to smile and laugh to defuse a
situation, or to underscore your points in making a case for
yourself. Just as you should never take "no" personally,
try not to take yourself so seriously that you
act defensive in the face of criticism.

ᒍOIE-ISM #3

Look for the greater potential
in the narrow opportunities presented to you.
My agreeing to speak to groups of spouses at conventions may
have seemed like a dead-end task, but I realized this could be a
doorway to gaining access for selling advertising
in *Broward Life Magazine* to their husbands.

CHAPTER TWO

Perseverance Pays Off

JOIE-ISM #4

It's rare you get what you want or need on the first try.
Don't take no as a personal rejection.
You must realize that no often means you simply haven't shown
the value yet of what you have to offer.

When you look at the degree of change that can happen in just one person's lifetime, you begin to understand why you really can't put restrictions on yourself at any stage of life. My grandma Rose was born before 1900, before Kitty Hawk and the Wright Brothers, and she rode around in a horse and carriage. By the time she died in 1975, she was flying back and forth on planes to Florida. These unexpected changes and opportunities illustrate how the limits you have on your life are mostly the ones you're setting on yourself.

There have been so many times in my own life when somebody said to me "no, that's not going to happen," and then it got really interesting when their idea of no wasn't my idea of no. It depends on how much you want to accomplish something and how wide-open your vision is to opportunity. For instance, all sorts of people take up painting when they're older and they absolutely love it and they create some phenomenal stuff. People do things with silk, or woodworking, all sorts of mediums.

It doesn't have to involve something artistic. Let's say it's just about an attitude that you decide to cultivate. When I wake up in the morning, I always do some kind of prayer thanking God for the beautiful day, whether it's raining or not. I will find something wonderful simply because I am here, I am alive, and I have been given the gift of this day.

People who say they don't want to get out of bed before 10 or 11 o'clock should realize that's an attitude placing limitations on yourself. If you absolutely want to do that as a conscious choice, there is nothing wrong with getting out of bed at that time. But if you feel like you're in a rut, you can change that state of mind and begin your approach to experiencing each new day.

You're the one who has the power and the ability to get yourself out of a rut. If you like to wake up and drink coffee, start by trying a different place to have your coffee. Have you ever bought a different type of coffee? Have you made your coffee differently using a different coffee-maker? Have you added a new flavor to it? Have you invited someone over to have coffee with you? Your list may have only one minor change, but your list of changes to get out of a self-imposed rut could be endless.

For me, even in the years I have spent in so-called retirement, I always regard whatever year it is as the best one of my life. I really find it to be true. If you're always discovering new things and developing new interests, it can always be the best year of your life. Depending on how you perceive yourself, you're either going to create a great life for yourself and enjoy yourself every day, or you will stay in a rut and that rut can become a canyon. You have an active choice in how you spend your time.

During the Great Depression, millions of people were in ruts, particularly financial ruts. Jobs were hard to come by. My father got a job by holding a package over his head navigating his way through the crowds applying for this one particular job, until he squeezed his way up to the head of the line.

If you knew my dad, whom I called "Pop", this was astounding, as he was a rather shy man. But he just needed a job. He needed to get out of that rut. He took the package and kept telling people along the line that he had to deliver it: "I have a package for Mr. So and So." Mr. So and So was the person everybody was trying to see about the job. Once my father got close to him, he admitted, "It's really not a package meant for you, but it means everything to me that I get this job." And he got the job! I may have perceived Pop as someone who is not so assertive, but that story about him inspired me many times because it illustrated how perseverance and resourcefulness can get you where you need to go, especially if it's out of a rut in life.

Always Take Your Goal Seriously, Not Yourself

Having the experience of being the key person for closing a real estate deal in Maryland worth more than ten million dollars was truly a once in a lifetime moment. I had been talking to brokers and lawyers every day for ten months, all of whom were bombarding me with requests that I should, as the seller representative, agree to be liable forever if certain things occurred. Well, NO WAY!

I was representing three estates and my strongest selling point was how this deal had to care for the widows, children and relatives of the deceased for generations to come. I could not compromise on either the price or the terms.

Since these brokers and lawyers involved in the deal always spoke on the phone with me, no one knew what I looked like. I was so insistent and persistent in pushing my objectives they must have thought I was a seven-foot-tall person who could play great basketball! Not the case. I am a fraction over five foot, and even with high heels and red hair pouffed up, I still wouldn't reach five foot five inches.

When I walked into the conference room for the closing meeting wearing a St John knit suit with a gold trimmed white collar, black and gold metallic jacket buttons, and clicking my high heels, a noticeable gasp went up from the men around the table. I placed a small gold opaque gift bag in front of each of them. They, of course, were perplexed. No one brings a souvenir gift to a closing! Then I took my place at the head of the long table. Later, I was told that they expected me to be much "taller," or at least "bigger" than I was.

We were almost concluded when a lawyer to my left loudly asked for the umpteenth time in the negotiations if I would agree to the ongoing liability clause. "NO," I said firmly, but not too loudly, as I did not want to embarrass him. I was pretty surprised that the subject had even come up again.

"Well, you're a tough cookie," he remarked.

"Cookie? Cookie? Did someone say 'cookie'? I would love a cookie!"

My response got tension relieving laughter from the group, and of course, I wasn't taking myself too seriously just because this guy had to keep hammering away on behalf of his client's wishes, while probably charging some hefty hourly rate.

Shortly afterwards we concluded the deal, signed all of the papers, and I instructed everyone to please open their gift. It was a figurine of a curled-up adorable red fox that resembled the logo of the property being sold, which was known as Fox Rest.

Now we could rest and the Fox property could rest. I hoped that all of the new owners would be at peace and enjoy this property as much as my Dad and the other two estate owners had, all of whom would have fainted at the selling price. But it was a property key to the purchase of other apartment buildings in the area. You know what they say about real estate. It's location, location, location that adds greatly to its value.

For me, the lesson from this experience was I should always take my goal seriously, but don't take myself too seriously. To be persistent, yet be able to be flexible and roll with the humor and make the best of any situation, even one where I would never budge.

Early Days in Florida

In the early days of my career, they made you wait a year to sit for your real estate licensing exam in Florida, so as I waited to take the exam, I took jobs selling advertising. First for *The Broward Review*, the local legal newspaper which at the time had one column of classified advertising. I learned about display advertisements which were the ads with a box around them. They had very few of those, so I asked if I could focus on selling more of those. I also asked to attend and report on the Broward Trial Lawyers Association.

"Oh, we don't cover that."

"Well, you do now." I thought it would be a great way to meet people since I was so new to Florida. I would go to the dinners and met several of what turned out to be my best new friends. All of the attendees at these dinner meetings were men. An unexpected benefit was meeting future judges and people who were key in county law enforcement. Several of these lawyers seemed to enjoy that I wanted to report on their meetings for the legal newspaper.

I soon caught the attention of the *Fort Lauderdale News* as now *The Broward Review* had increased its classified advertising from one column to one page and now also had a noticeable amount of display advertising. They expected you to stay in the office and generate sales from your desk. The *Fort Lauderdale News* offered me a job selling advertising with similar office parameters, but my daughter was very young and I wanted more flexibility to be there when she got home from school, so I sold advertising for a small weekly newspaper in Davie, Florida, near where I lived. With that job I could make my own appointments and manage my own time. I expanded their circulation to closer to where I lived and kind of maxed out their territory.

Every Monday I would have a route that would take me down a certain part of western Broward County, where I'd stop by the same places pretty much at the same time each week. On Mondays around 2 p.m., I would be at this country club in Plantation. There was one man there in charge of advertising and he would be the one to approve their ads. For about three weeks I went by on Mondays and showed him the newspaper and he always said no, he wasn't interested in placing an ad.

When I went the fourth week, instead of walking into his office, I just tossed the paper inside and he got up in a big mad huff and snapped at me, "I wouldn't wrap a fish in that newspaper. Please don't come back."

I didn't take offense and the next week, since I was in the neighborhood anyway, I went to the country club. I knocked on his doorframe, but because the door was open, I went ahead and said, "Hi, how are you Bob? Have you changed your mind about my newspaper?"

"I won't advertise in your newspaper! And I don't think it makes any sense for you to come back!"

But the next week, I went back anyway and tossed the latest edition of the newspaper into his office. He got up really mad, and blurted, "I told you don't come back! I wouldn't wrap a fish in that newspaper!"

So I thought, *okay, give it a break*. I didn't go by his office for a few weeks. Then I got a phone call from him asking, "Where have you been?"

"I thought you didn't want me to come by anymore."

"If you're in the neighborhood come on by, I kind of miss you." We both laughed.

The next time I went by I said to him, "Look Bob, how about if I offer you a six-inch column ad and you can put in information about your Sunday brunch? If you don't get any response to a specific ad, I will refund every penny."

That was more than fair, so he agreed. He got a good response to the ad and the most wonderful irony, or the most wonderful news, was he wound up advertising in our newspaper every single week after that, and took out bigger and bigger ads.

To me this story illustrates not only the importance of persistence, but of using personality and humor in a way that is effective. Someone else may be more dignified or more sophisticated, or more something than I was, but by throwing the paper in his office and him getting so irate, I got a different response out of him. He got so used to me coming around that when I stopped, he felt something was missing from his Monday afternoons.

I was able to make that offer about refunding him if it didn't work simply because every local print publication at that time had lots of extra column inches or spaces available for advertising. Many times our paper would run public service ads, or we would trade our ad space for something. There was always available space, so I knew I wasn't really making such a gigantic offer because if he didn't take it, the space would always be filled with something else.

While working with this small newspaper, I created new ways of doing things. There was one strip center with 13 small stores. I went into each store and said to the owners, "How would you like to have a full-page ad in this newspaper? How about the back page?" And they would invariably say we're a small store, we can't do a full page. "If I can get the other people in the shopping center to participate, would you participate?" And every one of them said sure.

I wound up selling 13 weeks of a full-page ad because I had each of the 13 shop owners reserve a two by three column inch space in the ad. The carrot that sold it was every week we would feature an article in the center of the page about one individual store. We published pictures of the owners, quoted them, and added customer testimonials. That was a big hit with those 13 businesses who otherwise couldn't afford a full page individually.

Eventually I had 112 active accounts in the western part of Broward County. I felt like I had sold everybody in that newspaper's circulation area. It was maxed out. There was another publication, a full-color magazine on the eastern side of the county called *Gold Coast Pictorial* and I thought, *I have 112 accounts, why don't I go see them about working for them.*

I made an appointment and saw their vice president in charge of sales, and asked him for a job selling advertising. I told him I already had 112 accounts in west Broward County, I wouldn't require a salary, and could just work on commission.

It never occurred to me they wouldn't want me to work for them. Surprise, surprise, he said, and I quote, "We don't want *those* people. We have a fine society publication and our salespeople are used to making $300 a week."

To me $300 a week was a significant amount of money at that time. I didn't think I'd have any problem doing that because I was good at sales, but he hemmed and hawed about hiring me. I even said to him, "Are you sure you don't want to hire me to sell advertising?"

I couldn't believe it because I had been so good at advertising sales ever since high school. When I was advertising manager of our yearbook and sold so much advertising that I had to stop to leave enough room for the graduation photos. But this guy wasn't buying my offer. I got the impression he just didn't want to expand his circulation to the western part of the county. *Those* people he was referring to were new arrivals to Broward County from the Northeast, many from New York, and at that time Broward County was growing by leaps and bounds. It was the fastest growing county in the United States. Most of the growth, however, was in the western part of the county.

I left his office really perplexed. When I walked outside and stood in front of their building, I felt as if I had been in a movie portraying this young woman with her arms raised to the sky, saying aloud, "If that's the competition, I am going to do my own magazine!"

I went back home, totally stunned. I said to my then boyfriend, "I really think I could start a magazine for this part of the county. I already have all these ad accounts and could convert them. Why don't I publish my own magazine?"

He asked me what I would need to start such a venture. I really had no idea. In those days $10,000 seemed like the most enormous amount of money I could think of, so I said, "I think I'd need $10,000." He looked at me, this very successful man, and said, "Are you sure you wouldn't rather have a bracelet?"

And I said no, "I really think that there is a need for a magazine for our part of the county and I don't see why I can't just do it."

After our conversation, the magazine we called *Inverrary Life* was born; Inverrary being a real estate development in the western part of the county. The Inverrary golf tournament was nationally televised, and the comedian Jackie Gleason lived in the community, so it was an established neighborhood and destination.

The timing for the magazine turned out to be terrific because the existing county magazine had no interest in that market. I worked very hard all summer on getting this magazine off the ground. The target date for the first publication was in October.

We engaged Don Shula, coach of the Miami Dolphins professional football team, to be our first cover subject.

Talking Don Shula Out of "No"

The person I had found to be editor for the magazine was from the same place in Ohio as Miami Dolphins' football coach Don Shula—he even knew somebody who worked with Shula. We contacted his public relations firm and got him to agree to be on our first cover. Then I went out and started to convert the 112 ad accounts I had by touting that Shula, head coach of the World Champion Miami Dolphins, who was a very big name in South Florida, would be on our first cover.

We had a writer who was also the editor, my first and longtime assistant and secretary Brenda, and myself—the three of us were really it for the magazine when we first started out. Eventually, we added an art director and she worked part-time to put the magazine together and create the ads. We worked out of an apartment in the west part of Broward County. I got a lot of good advertisers and we got some good articles and were really ready to go preparing our first issue. Then the football strike happened.

We were told by Shula's publicist that he wouldn't be able to be on the cover simply because he was totally involved in the football strike. He was a towering figure not only in football, but in the nation. He had to be one of the most outstanding people you could have to grace the first cover of a magazine. This was initially a big disappointment, but I just wasn't going to accept he would say no after he had told us yes, especially since we had predicated so many ad sales based on him being on the cover.

Somehow, I wangled the phone number of the Miami Dolphins' locker room, from where Coach Shula was said to be involved in negotiating this football strike contract. I got through and asked to speak to him. But they weren't letting me anywhere near him, so I had to say I was a personal friend of the family and it was urgent that I talk to him. I was very persistent.

Finally, I got Don Shula on the phone and told him of our situation and how he had promised to be on the cover and there was no way he now could not be. I offered him all sorts of ways of doing it easily and insisted "There's no way you're not going to be on the cover." He was still reluctant.

"Mr. Shula, we have sold all of this advertising based on your agreement to be on the first cover of *Inverrary Life* magazine and we can't renege on all those people. You simply have to do this. I understand you're very busy with the football strike so here is what I propose. You get your public relations people to take some pictures of you that have not been published before and printed anywhere. We will send a list of questions and then you answer the questions when you have time with your public relations people and that will suffice."

He hesistated and finally said, "I just don't know if I can spare the time."

I gave it one last shot. "Mr. Shula, if you're negotiating a strike, do you think when somebody gives their word in your negotiations that they should keep it, or, are you okay with them backing off it? We have nothing stronger than our word. That's who we are. Without your personal integrity, who are you? You agreed to this and we're counting on you. Other people are counting on you, and we've given you options for an easy way to get it done."

It was then and still is to this day really important to me that when a person gives their word, that's who they are, and they don't renege on their word. If you can't do something, you have to renegotiate it: my dad taught me when I was a little girl that if you say you're going to do something, you do it. If you find for some reason you can't, then you have to renegotiate, you can't just walk away from the agreement or forget about it. If somebody promises to do something, or tells me they are going to do something for me or with me, and then they don't do it, my opinion of them changes.

Don Shula got my point and he finally agreed to cooperate with us, becoming our first magazine cover, which was a big hit and launched our new publication.

Don't Take No for an Answer

It took us from June to October to put out the first issue of my *Inverrary Life* magazine. I was absolutely stunned, oh wow, we have to do this again and again. The November issue was a sort of hodgepodge of the same sort of thing and I realized that if this magazine was to survive and grow, I better do more with it. So I had this wild thought to go to New York and sell national advertising for our brand new publication.

I wrote to a few ad agencies after picking advertisers I liked. One of them was J&B Scotch, which was sometimes my drink of choice in those years. I thought they would be ideal for us because in those days they did a Christmas jingle bells ad which I wanted in our December issue.

I persisted in finding the right guy to speak with in New York, got an appointment, and went into this man's office. I showed him the magazine and he responded very nicely and politely with, "I can't advertise here. Your magazine is tiny and we only advertise in primary markets. South Florida is not even a secondary market. It's a tertiary market."

This was the first time I had ever heard the expression tertiary market. I really wasn't listening to him and replied, "You have to do this. It will be so exciting for people to see your ad in this magazine."

But he insisted, "I really don't think I can do it."

"You know what," I persisted, "the amount of money you have in your Christmas promotional fund, a fraction of it would pay for a cover in my magazine, and you have such a big budget, and you place so much importance with where you're placing your ads, I don't even know why you're talking to me. So I'll tell you what: I'll give you my FedEx account number, you just send the ad to me, and I will run it on a cover of the December issue."

"I'm trying to tell you I can't do that."

"Why can't you?"

"Because it's just not a big enough market and we just don't do publications that small."

I tried another approach. "Everyone knows that South Florida is sophisticated with great theatre and musicals."

"No it isn't!" he objected.

"You're absolutely right. Everyone loves to party and drink and so your Scotch will make a huge impact when they see your ad in an unexpected place!"

He laughed.

I persisted. "This might be an eye-opening trial run for you because if you put this ad in *Time* magazine, people will see it and just turn the page because they expect it to be there. You put this ad in my magazine in South Florida, people will stare at it, they will wonder how in the hell did this ad get in this magazine. How did they get J&B Scotch to advertise? Whoa! That's really amazing."

He laughed again, but this time accepted a piece of paper with my FedEx number written on it. I said, "Just send it and we'll give you the best placement. It's a big deal to us, but it's not going to be a big deal to you."

It was maybe $600 for an inside front cover of our magazine, which was not a big expense for a company with a huge ad budget like his. He smiled at me and said, "I admire your guts."

"I'll be looking for the ad and I need it by next week because we want to be sure you have the inside cover and I don't want to put anyone else there."

He laughed again and waved to me as I left his office. Sure enough, within the next week, a beautiful Jingle Bells-themed ad from J&B Scotch arrived. We ran it on the inside cover of the December edition, which was our third issue. We had our first national advertising in this little publication called *Inverrary Life* Magazine (soon to become *Broward Life Magazine*).

The magazine kept growing and was really well received as we worked on building a larger circulation. We had inserts in all the magazines, we sent out direct mail to solicit subscriptions, and many times we copied names off mailboxes and would stick things next to people's doors promoting the publication.

One of the people I met was a man in charge of advertising for a large bank in Fort Lauderdale, called Landmark Bank. He gave me some great advice. "I really like your magazine, but Inverrary is a small development in the western part of the county. If you would change the name to something bigger, then I could advertise."

"What would you like to call it?"

He said we could name it for the county. "How about if you called it *Broward Life*?"

"Consider it done," I said. "We'll change the name and I look forward to having your ad, but you have to buy a lot of covers from us because we're changing the name for you."

He went along with that and regularly bought advertising for his bank.

Lots of people told me you can't change the name of a publication once it is launched. Really? Why can't you? So many things that people arbitrarily say you can't do, or say won't work, should just be ignored. Do what you think you need to do, go for it, do the work, and see what you can make happen.

We changed the name without any problem at all. Then, as we were growing because we had a bigger name, we were able to expand into other parts of Broward County. By the May 1975 issue, *Broward Life Magazine* reflected readership across the entire county, and as a result our advertising and subscription success really took off.

When Persistence Means Finding Something

Sometimes not taking "no" for an answer isn't about selling something, but about finding something. My company, JMG Publishing, once had a printing job for a bank's annual report, and the look of it was quite understated. The cover was the bank's logo blind embossed, along with some gold leaf to highlight the bank's name.

We were very proud of the design and were about to deliver the 5,000 copies that had been ordered. Almost at the point of finishing the job I was surprised to get a phone call requesting that we increase the order to 10,000 copies. That seemed wonderful until I had to locate more paper for the cover. It was a heavyweight stock in a deep forest green with a beautiful texture and a pattern within the paper. It was an understandably spectacular paper, and it really set the tone for the entire report.

Without giving it much thought, I dialed my paper supplier who told me they were out of that paper. "Are you out of it in Miami, or are you out of it in the world?" He answered, "I'm sorry, we just can't get anymore."

Tracking down the mill, it turned out it was a Strathmore paper, and I contacted the mill that same day. "We have no more of that particular stock," I was told. I supposed we could have used something else, but it would never have looked the same, so I ventured to ask, "Where did you sell your last big order?" They told me that a company in Texas had purchased a very large order but they doubted I would be able to get any of it.

Not one to be easily dissuaded, I called the printing company in Texas and told them what I needed. They informed me they had enough offcut (which is the stock that remains after the job is completed, and usually is discarded if it isn't a large amount) to finish our job but it would be very heavy to send it to Florida. I gave them my FedEx account number and asked them to ship it fast.

The stock arrived and we were able to finish the job without the client ever knowing. The shipping cost, of course, was figured into the new additional copies and everyone was pleased. A win-win occurred because the first "no" really didn't matter. All it took was persistence to discover that yes, there still was some of that paper left in the world!

Always Persist in Protecting What You Most Love

Have you heard of anyone having a "pet tree"? I had one! Oliver was an olive tree so beautiful that the first time I drove past him, I had to back up and look again. I was at a nursery in Palm Springs, California, and my "magic house" condo had an open inside atrium with a dirt floor. Seemed like a great place for a personal tree.

When they delivered Oliver, they insisted on leaving him outside. That would never do, so when my neighbor's landscapers arrived, I asked, and they agreed to move Oliver inside. Only problem was they needed a specific kind of heavy-duty moving device. While we were discussing this, a truck pulled up to take a couch I was donating to their charity. Lo and behold, they had a suitable moving device, and the driver was a doll in helping the landscapers bring Oliver inside.

The landscapers had to come back later in the day to plant him, but soon Oliver had his own room and was happily growing in the condo. When I moved out of this condo, Oliver just had to come with me, and he was soon transported by crane (another guy who initially thought I was nuts!) to an ideal spot in the garden area of my next desert home. When I moved again, I insisted that Oliver had to come along. This time we created a special spot for him worthy of his status as one of the most famous trees in the Palm Springs area.

All the landscapers in the area repeated stories of this crazy lady and her pet olive tree! Alas, when I left Palm Springs, those landscapers said they could not truck him to Carmel Valley. "Well, what kind of truck do you need?" I asked. I rented one and we drove in tandem to the new house.. I had already met the landscapers for the new house, since I was going to use the same people as the previous owner. I called the head guy Sergio and he said, "No way anyone in my crew is going to plant an olive tree on a Sunday. They're all at a picnic."

It was rare, if not unheard of, to move a tree so many times, and I explained to Sergio that Oliver would be arriving, and simply had to be planted or he could die. "Can you please encourage your men? I am happy to pay them extra." I could almost see Sergio scratching his head while trying to convince me that what I wanted was impossible. Since I had done stuff like this more than once, I just persisted. When we arrived, Sergio had promised nothing, but he and four guys were there to greet Oliver and they carefully and lovingly planted him. But I knew then that I could not move him again. He had to be trimmed and coddled, and we placed special rocks and stones and toys that a tree would like, and hoped for the best.

All of the guys were quite macho and really did not want to do a group hug with Oliver in the center. Some really good Mexican beer persuaded them otherwise and we all formed a circle around Oliver and hugged him and each other. They ultimately loved the experience, and we all enjoyed many a laugh about it for all the years I lived there. Oliver is still there, and the new owners of that house love him too. Debbie made him a beautiful ceramic sign with his name, and he still wears it proudly.

Don't be afraid to persist when you really care about something, as I have learned that the other people involved may soon feel good about it too. They may never expect to enjoy the experience and go from thinking you are nuts to enjoying working for you and retelling stories about your own Oliver.

Scaling the Mountains of Life

I first took up hiking in Palm Springs on Mt. San Jacinto. It was exhilarating to me to experience inner peace outdoors, like on the top of a mountain! When I was living in the desert, and Lew was continuing to commute from the East Coast and spend some time out West, I became part of a core group that helped to expand a newly formed Southern California hiking club in the Coachella Valley, aptly called the Coachella Valley Hiking Club. I went on the radio and told people about this new club, and eventually, counting family members, we reached in excess of 1,000 members! I did our first newsletter, designed the logo and graphics for T-shirts.

We would ride up to the top on the tram and hike near the top of Mt. San Jacinto. There was one hike every year called the Cactus to Clouds Hike, where people started on the street and hoped to climb all the way to the peak of the mountain, which is 10,802 feet, and then walk back down to the street. A few guys who were built like gazelles accomplished that climb.

One year my friend Wendie and I decided we would climb from the street to the top of Mt. San Jacinto, but we decided not to tell anyone else in the hiking club. We trained quietly to get ourselves in shape to go up further and further. When the hike was scheduled, we announced we were going to do it too, and all the "gazelle hikers" looked at us like we were out of our minds.

Wendie and I winked at each other and started climbing. We stuck with the group and got to the point where some people decided to turn around. The hike leaders looked at us thinking we would probably be in that quitter group, but we shook our heads, no.

We kept going until Wendie and I made it to the top. We were so excited. They give you a badge signifying that you had summited—it's a whole big deal. Then we walked back halfway down to the tram station and took the tram down. It was 11 or 12 miles of hiking and when we got down to the ground I called my friend Rick, who was one of my hiking inspirations, and Philip, who was the founder of the hiking club; I was yelling into the phone, "We did it, we did it!" There was no one who would have ever thought Wendie and I could have climbed that mountain, but we had the confidence, the persistence, and we kept each other inspired.

If you put your mind to something, who says you can't do it? Put one foot in front of the other and you will get there. You might not be the first person there, but so what. The whole thing boils down to your own belief that you can do something. Like the Henry Ford quote, "If you think you can, or you think you can't, you're right." We really believed we could do it and we did it!.

Many lifelong friendships were formed during my hiking club period, and the metaphors for learning were endless. We did a hike in the Indian Canyons where I learned a big lesson. We came to an opening on the trail (a chasm to me) that was more than two feet wide. When I looked down, yikes, it was a long drop into a canyon. Our hike leader and a person who taught me so much,

Rick, told me how to put one foot out, and where to place the other. He promised he would be there to catch me if necessary, but assured me I would make it over just fine. Now I grant you that Rick was over six feet tall, a well-built guy who could climb anything; and I was barely an inch over five feet. I hesitated and hesitated, stuck there for a very long time. "No, I'll go back. See you guys later," and similar mutterings continued to pour out of my mouth.

Rick settled me down, while others behind me weren't all so brave either. But he had patience, and finally I squeezed my eyes shut and just did it. I thought it was impossible, but he thought it was probable.

What I was thinking was creating my reality, a type of learning that I describe more fully later in this book. He also taught me on another hike how to fall and land without getting injured. What?! I wasn't ever thinking I would need to learn how to fall, but he insisted this was a valuable thing to know.

A story that may not have made me infamous, but definitely legendary in the world of desert hiking, happened on my first hike with the Coachella Valley Hiking Club. I was all excited to have gone to an outdoor store owned by one of the members and purchased my first boots, Merrell's, which have now been bronzed and sit as a welcome to anyone coming in my front door! The bronzing was a surprise gift from a dear jeweler friend in Palm Desert who nicknamed me The Rustic Princess.

I also got a backpack, a jacket and an adventure hat, and was ready. I signed up for a hike on Murray Peak, which was an eight-miler, and took off with the others. What they didn't know was that I was wearing nylons under some colorful pants that I had found at the Encinitas Street Fair. What a fashion statement! Colorful wild patches on my pants, hiking boots, a big tan hat, and a large backpack with lunch in it to complete the outfit.

What I never realized was that as you climb higher, you get hotter. Yikes, it was a scorcher of a day and I was doing my best to keep up. Some of the hikers were very experienced and were soon barely visible to me. I kept going and had some pals with me as we trudged along. Finally, I said I had to go behind some desert shrubbery and lose the nylons.

Nylons! They couldn't believe it. Who wears nylons on a hike? The hiking club never let me forget my first foray on the trails of Palm Springs. That story was told at every event. Thank goodness I wrote the newsletter, or otherwise it would have appeared in print for them to chuckle at over and over again. It was still laughed about for all the years I lived there.

If there is a moral to this story, it is "Go for it." Who cares that you may not know all the best ways to do something, but if you are up for trying it, and you have a sense of humor and can laugh at yourself, then there is a lot of fun out there for you to experience; even when you don't expect crazy outcomes. What I also gained was finding a wonderful new bunch of friends.

Today my frequent hiking buddy is someone I met through the Center for Spiritual Living, Napa Valley. We both love the texture and stillness of the redwood trees as we silently trudge up the trails near creeks and other magnificent expressions of nature. David is a highly skilled photographer and we delight in finding picturesque compositions. He sees potential in so many ordinary arrangements of leaves and rocks. It's a joy for me to feel the peace and serenity of being in and breathing in what nature provides.

Discovering nature is discovering another world, and I soak it up absolutely loving every minute. My introduction to this changed my life in many spiritual ways and also gave me a physical courage I was not aware of possessing.

When I went to my high school fiftieth reunion, we spent time in that same elementary school where I had introduced Eleanor Roosevelt. There was something we had in that school's gym called the "monkey club." Kids in my class who could climb overhanded up a rope to the top were qualified to be members of the monkey club. I could never get off the ground with that rope.

At this reunion I went back to that gym and pulled one of the ropes out to see if I could get up any higher. I was determined, I had the courage, but I still couldn't do it. After all of that time, I was still thinking *I've got to try this monkey club again*. I've always been so determined to succeed, and perseverance remains one of the trademarks of my life.

Always remember, while you don't always win, and you don't always get to where you want to go, there is nothing wrong with giving it a try . . . at any age.

JOIE-ISM #5

If you give yourself a million reasons not to do something,
you can absolutely paralyze yourself with fears and concerns.
I didn't really know I couldn't start a magazine,
so I just forged ahead and didn't worry.

JOIE-ISM #6

Your word really matters.
Without integrity, who are you? What do you really have?
Whatever you're doing, however small the commitment might be,
or however great, keep your word.

CHAPTER THREE

Trust Your Intuition

You don't have to know and understand the whole process.
Just have a goal in mind. Start somewhere and trust the Universe.
Expect to feel guided. Follow the zigzags feeling confident they will
lead you to something or to where you need to be.

Have you ever asked yourself, *should I do this?* And some inner voice shouts back a big *YES!* Or do you sense within yourself that it's okay to give something a try, despite what others have advised?

Trusting your intuition, your inner wisdom, is a key to success, and you need to learn to follow it. You have so many layers of consciousness, so many levels of awareness and sensing. Someone who performs really well has often learned to enter an intuitive zone at will. It's a sense of trusting and knowing there is an ability within themselves that is so much greater than what they even think is possible.

Giving careful thought, coupled with intuition, to the skills of the people you hire or choose to work with, usually can put the odds in your favor for a good result. If you are not yet sure of trusting your own instincts about a person, ask someone else who you trust to interview them, or ask that person sit in when you interview the job candidate. I have a peculiar experience with this to share as an illustration.

My dog Pretzel became so adept at signaling bad choices in employees that we jokingly promoted her to Vice President in Charge of Personnel. We even printed up some business cards for her. For example, Pretzel was spot-on when we had to hire a guy to run a new press at my printing plant. We needed a person with specific experience and skills at running this particular press, and a guy who sounded like a perfect fit was referred to us.

We started off well in interviewing him, but I was shocked to see my small Maltese dog angrily tugging at the cuff of his jeans. I found myself apologizing and making excuses for Pretzel. I hired the man and he started right away on the night shift. His second night on the job, I got a call from the night manager saying either this new guy had to be fired, or all of the other employees would be unhappy. Just like that, we realized that Pretzel had this man's personality pegged.

I didn't know anyone else who could operate that particular press, so I had to keep him on, but the situation worsened. Finally, I realized that this guy had to go. He made some noise about getting his union involved—we were not a union shop—and I wasn't sure how to proceed.

Sometimes strange situations call for doing things "outside the nine dots." Remember that saying? It meant that in order to connect the nine dots (three rows of three dots) you had to draw a line outside the dots and then, without lifting your pencil, draw a line back to the dot that needed connecting. I mention this because the "outside the nine dots" resolution that I came up with was to sell the press. No press, no job.

Even the union he wanted to get involved had to go along with my decision on that option. The press was sold, and another new more sleek and modern one took its place. A great new guy that everyone, including Pretzel, liked learned to run that press, and we were careful to always be sure from then on that whomever we hired had to be a good personality fit for our crew.

It was important to me that my employees enjoyed their jobs and anything the company could do to create a fun and pleasant working environment was well worth the effort. Your success depends on your employees. You can't do it alone, so create conditions where everyone gets along and enjoys their work. That is a win-win and everyone succeeds. We also definitely trusted Pretzel's canine intuition thereafter every time we were considering new hires!

Do Women have an Intuition Advantage?

Our culture tends to stereotype and generalize about many subjects, including whether women are more intuitive than men. I don't know that women are more in tune with their intuition than men. I certainly haven't seen evidence of it.

Any preconceived notion of what you're supposed to be doing can cloud your interpretation of intuitive messages you receive. Maybe in this regard women have traditionally had more preconceived notions forced upon them by our culture, based on what was expected of us in playing gender roles.

Whether you are a man or woman, when your intuition fails you it's usually because you are pushing it away. You aren't allowing your real inner guidance to come through because you're engaged in self-doubt that undermines trust in your intuition. You must stand up for yourself and say I want this and not that. But first you must really know what it is you truly want. That is mostly an intuitive process and it's a big obstacle for many people because they really don't know what it is they want.

When you're in tune with your own intuition and open and receptive, you can find signs of it everywhere. When you are open to asking the Universe, signs will come to point the way on what your next step could be. If someone offers you a book to read, for example, read it, even if it doesn't make sense for you at the time. It could be a symbol of taking a different route. Maybe it's divine guidance. If you look at a restaurant menu and see something you have never tried before, go for it. It's like the menu of life. How limiting it is if you keep ordering the same thing.

Sometimes intuition means you have to know when not to say something and wait for a more opportune time to have a conversation with another person. You have to come from a place of seeking improvement in a situation because most of us are hardwired to react defensively to criticism. Be smart enough to know (by putting yourself in someone else's shoes) their point of view in order for you to have the impact you desire.

One reason why I speak from experience about the intuitiveness of men is that most of my best friends, my entire life, have been men, though I have had wonderful friends who were women. Maybe it was because I had been so close to my father when I was a child. As a result, I just haven't seen any evidence that women are more sensitive or more intuitive than the men I've known.

Many of these platonic relationships with men formed through falling in love with hiking and being outdoors, admiring the beauty of nature. As mentioned in an earlier chapter, when I was living in Palm Springs, a lot of my best friends were men who became my hiking buddies. (My husband hiked with me too, and we once climbed Mount Wilson in Arizona on an 11-mile hike. He often prefers golf these days.)

My hiking buddies included Ralph, a retired L.A. Sheriff's Deputy, Frank, a retired PG&E lineman, and Sheldon, who had worked in the investment industry on the East Coast. Beyond hiking, we had little in common, but we still became great friends due to the joy we got from being outdoors and being physically active. That was a common thread for many of my new friends then. My friend, Wendie, a nurse and part owner of a medical equipment company, was part of this group too. Most of us were grandparents and we called ourselves The Mixed Trail Nuts. I eventually became a state parks volunteer for 13 years at Point Lobos State Natural Reserve in Carmel, California (more about that later) and also volunteered at Muir Woods in Mill Valley.

The retired deputy, in particular, became my fast friend even though we were so different. We were once in the Indian Canyons in Palm Springs listening to a rare waterfall trickle, and I said to Ralph, "Can you feel the spirit of the Native Americans who lived here?"

"No," he said, and followed that with, "Joie, you're nuts."

I shared with him what I had learned about astrology and the concept of Mercury retrograde, which is the belief that during those times when this planet appears to travel in reverse, communication and mechanical breakdowns are more likely to occur. Again, "Joie, you're nuts." He said that a lot.

As our friendship grew we both came to know that we could count on the other to be there if ever needed at 4:00 am. Ralph pushed me kindly in ways I didn't think I could manage. He would say, "You can dooooo it, Joieeeee," as he encouraged me to climb higher, be stronger, hike further, crawl through all sorts of muck and yuck, and feel safer than I ever had. I miss Ralph. I was probably one of the last people he spoke to when I visited him in the hospital before he transitioned to the next life of his soul.

For our paths to cross and create such joy, we had to all share a common love of hiking. If you want to meet more like-minded people, I suggest it would be great to find something you are interested in and meet others who share your interest. Classes, sports, dancing, Qigong, whatever. When you don't think you have an idea as to what would interest you, close your eyes and picture an event or events when you felt really happy. That could be a great clue as to what it is you really enjoy.

Sometimes we are so constricted by what we are supposed to like that we doubt something so far afield from it would attract us. One of my favorite quotes is by the poet e.e. cummings when he wrote: "It takes courage to grow up and turn out to be who you really are." I have a framed graphic of that quote sitting above my computer, and am looking at it as I write these words.

Go for it, try something new, or think about something in a new way. It could relate to anything: your job, your career, your hobbies, your relationships, your family, your place of worship, or whatever else you can imagine. Anything can be expanded and looked at differently. Discover your true calling, your true enjoyments. Yes, "You CAN do it!"

Serendipity and Intuition Go Together

Fully engaging your intuition enables you to sense and seize opportunities, often in the most unexpected ways and under the most challenging of circumstances.

In June 1966, my first husband Michael and I separated, as I feared I would continue living a programmed life that really didn't suit me. He was from Long Island and I was from Westchester County, New York. His dad was a wonderful doctor, his mother was a doll, but it just wasn't the life I wanted. It was all about who you were having dinner with, what you wore, when your next tennis match was?

It was too small of a life for me and I wanted a divorce. In those days in New York the only reason for granting a divorce was adultery. But they were still honoring what was called a Mexican divorce, so I had a lawyer arrange for me to get a divorce in Mexico.

I was told to fly to El Paso and stay in a particular hotel, and the next morning an attorney named Luis would be looking for me in the lobby. He'd then take me to the courthouse. That made perfect sense.

On the plane down to El Paso I sat next to a man from New York who just looked at me and asked, "Freedom Flight?" I really didn't know what he meant. I thought I was the only person in the world going down there to get a divorce. His name was John and we became friends—we actually even dated for a while.

The next morning at the hotel I went downstairs and there were probably 400 people in the lobby. In the center of them was a man about five by five, wearing the biggest sombrero you've ever seen, blowing hard on a whistle. He looked like a giant top spinning around. He would whistle and then announce, "Line up and get in the buses."

There had to be ten buses waiting outside. I was like in shock that all of these people were getting divorces in Mexico that day. I thought I was the only one. Whoever piled into my bus started asking each other: "How many years?" It was like a game. A lot of people said 12, some people said five, or as many as 25. As for me, I had been married three years and nine months.

The bus caravan was rolling down this dirt road passing shacks, chicken coops, and navigating through an absolutely impoverished area of Juarez, Mexico. There wasn't a paved street in sight. Finally, we pulled up to a very large chicken coop, a single-story concrete and cinder block building, surrounded by chicken wire fence.

The wide short guy in the sombrero said to us, "Everybody out of the bus and line up." We were in the middle of nowhere. He blew his whistle again: "Line up in two lines." Passengers in the first bus lined up in two lines, then the next bus, and the next. When it was our turn we walked in twos into this nondescript building, through a doorway that was just an opening in a wall. We sat down on metal folding chairs, like you would find in a church basement, not knowing what to expect.

There was man behind a desk, a handsome man who looked like a young Omar Sharif. They started calling out names. When they called my name, I walked up and sat in a chair at this desk in front of "Omar Sharif," the judge who made decrees official. He did not say a word to me as I sat there. He had typewritten pages which he flipped through, and then with a fat red crayon signed his name with tight up and down strokes, and handed me the paper.

I was confused. "Am I divorced?"

He replied, "You no missus no more."

And that was it, the divorce was done. I got up, went back to my seat, and waited for the next bus to come in. Nobody talked to me. It was just crazy. The only reason they called your name was to give you the correct paper with your name on it. It was like a divorce factory. They just churned them out. I was one of the last people to get a Mexican divorce in November 1966 . Soon after New York no longer allowed it as a recognized divorce.

My friend John later took me to a restaurant in New York where he introduced me to escargot. I had never had them and fell in love with the delicacy. The Mexican divorce gave me a lagniappe (an unexpected gift) in the form of a love for escargot that to this day is still one of my favorite things to eat. Whenever Lew and I go to Paris, we eat a zillion escargot. It reminds me of France and it also reminds me in some ways of adventure, freedom, and trying something new.

Without realizing it as it happened, my divorce in 1966 was a big act of trailblazing, as few people I knew of were divorced in those days. Without some horrific reason for doing it, divorce was unheard of. I felt trapped in a life that many other people would have loved, but it just wasn't the life for me.

I am reminded of the David Whyte poem *"Sweet Darkness"* where the last line says: "Anything or anyone that does not bring you alive is too small for you." That thought has been guiding my life for a long time, even before I was aware it was a line in an eloquent poem. A copy of that poem sits above my desk today.

David Whyte is such a compelling and brilliant poet that I recommend you check out his work. He is able to touch your soul deeply with his pen, and his writing evokes for me heartfelt emotions and a big YES! One of his themes has been to connect spirituality and business. Now I more fully understand why I resonate with his work. Reading his poetry for me has been akin to an "aha" moment, and I always enjoy seeing him in person since the first time I met him in Palm Springs.

A far more cynical poet, T.S. Eliot, was a favorite of mine in college. I think *The Hollow Men* reminded me in some way of what I was trying to escape from when I chose not to live the programmed life of a young married woman in the early 1960s. That was a transformative decade for the entire country and perhaps I was feeling that energy on some level. I knew there had to be something bigger out there, something that created a sense of aliveness and purpose far beyond the mundane and comfortable.

Discovering My Love of Art

At the age of eight, in third grade, I was chosen to be one of three kids to paint a window in the newly created Halloween window painting contest in Scarsdale, New York. I was so excited we won first prize in our age group. I felt thrilled about it, but wouldn't let anyone know how much it mattered to me. It was the beginning of my love affair with art. It was a validation of my burgeoning love of art and of being an artist.

My dad had loved to paint, and he bought me my first paints when I was seven or eight. To this day I have his paint box with the original remnants of the Grumbacher oils he liked. It has become as valuable to me as any family heirloom.

When I was eleven, I had to drive for two hours with my mother to some long-lost place on Long Island, possibly East Hampton, to pick up a painting. She was involved in a charity that had received it as a donation, and had agreed to go pick it up. The ride was tedious, and when we finally arrived, she ran into the house to get the painting, while I was instructed to wait in the car. I did that for as long as I could, but was really antsy to walk around.

Once I ventured out of the car, I noticed a weather-beaten barn about fifty yards away. I shyly walked towards it and peered in. It was so memorable that I can still see it vividly to this day. On a tricycle sat a man with two paint buckets on each handlebar, and he was riding the tricycle and throwing down paint with a wide brush onto a canvas that was covering the floor. Whap! Zap! Spatter! The colors would just be thrown and flipped from a brush almost haphazardly as he continued pedaling. After about five minutes he turned around, as he must have sensed that someone was there. I was pressed against one side of the barn door opening. He didn't say a word and didn't smile. His stare made me feel uncomfortable so I scurried back to the car.

Years later, I learned that my mother had been talking to his wife, Lee Krasner, and had picked up the donated painting by none other than the famous Jackson Pollock. He never was known for being particularly friendly, but I realized later than I had seen something very special in the world of art. To this day, whenever I see a Pollock painting I can still see the roots of his technique, the splattering and paint throwing, and it makes me smile to know I witnessed a tiny bit of art history.

In the early 1960s, I was a teacher and went to a charity art show where I fell in love with this painting which today is over the fireplace in my living room. It is called "Fishing Boats at Night" by an artist named Leonardo Nierman. It cost me a whole month's salary, but I still love the way the light shines on it, the colors, and the movement in it.

After I bought that painting, I saw in *The New York Times* that Nierman would be doing a show at the Little Gallery in Philadelphia. That inspired me to write him a fan letter, which I have only done a few times in my entire life. I sent it to an address in Mexico and he sent me back a letter confirming he would be at the Little Gallery. I think he thought that because I lived in New York that Philadelphia was around the corner.

I took a train to Philadelphia and once I got to the gallery, there was no sign of him. The owner of the gallery told me Nierman had gotten sick and wasn't able to come, which was so disappointing since I had come all the way from New York. I wrote him another letter saying I went to the show and he wasn't there—he wrote back apologizing and sent along a book of his art work.

The next year, Jacqueline Kennedy bought his work and that's what really put him on the map. My painting tripled in value in a year. His background was in engineering, but he had developed this great unique artistic technique using splattered stars, fine lines and blotches.

Time passed and when Lew and I got married, we went to Mexico City on our honeymoon. This was 1980, and by then Leonardo Nierman had become very famous. I called his studio and made an appointment to see him the next day. When we shook hands, I said to him, do you remember in 1964 you had a show at the Little Gallery and didn't go because you were sick, and there was a lady from New York who loved your work and wrote you a letter? He nodded his head yes. "I am that lady." He grabbed me in a hug and said, "You're not a customer, you're a patron."

He was so excited and insisted that I get a sculpture and a painting for practically nothing. Later I sat with him and asked what I've always wanted to ask an artist: how do you know when a painting is finished?

He replied, "Sometimes I paint and paint and I just feel like this is the point to stop, it's done. But then there are other times I keep going and I just cock it up."

We established some kind of bond and I saw him again when I lived in Palm Springs. I reminded him again and oh yes, he once again responded with effusive hugs.

Serendipity Meets Intuition

As a very small child, up until the age of four, a great joy of mine was spending time with my Aunt Sylvia. She would pick me up at our apartment, take my small hand in hers, and we would walk outside along an area of flowers that bordered a tennis court. We continued walking up a steep hill to her building and once inside her apartment, I would be delighted by the smells of cookies, the magic of the colors that hung in paintings on the walls, and the sounds of her playing the piano and singing with me.

As it turned out, the painting behind her couch that made such an impression on me was a print of Renoir's "The Luncheon of the Boating Party." This painting came to symbolize Sylvia's role in my life, as I grew to love Renoir enough to visit his home in France, and to pursue a love of Impressionism. I would always say, "Renoir is my favorite." I didn't always remember why, but now I know it was that painting that I saw on my visits as a little girl, which left a lifelong "impression" on me.

Two months after my fourth birthday, Sylvia suddenly disappeared. "Where is Sylvia?" No one responded. My dad said he didn't know, but would tell me if he learned anything. My mother said, "I don't know but I heard she got shot in her eye," which is a pretty devastating thing to say to a child who is wistfully missing her aunt and quite distraught over her absence.

As time passed, I promised myself that one day I would find out what happened to her. Eventually, I learned the word "divorce" and came to realize that a component of that word in those days was to somehow banish the non-family member ex-spouses to oblivion, never to be spoken of again. That would never suffice for curious me, so I kept my promise and as I got older, continued to inquire about her, yet always without much result.

As an adult, I had an opportunity to ask a cousin that I rarely, if ever, saw to please ask his mother (another banished aunt due to divorce from my dad's other brother) if she knew what happened to Sylvia, as they were once friends. My cousin Robert's mother was a violinist of some accomplishment (her former husband, my Uncle Sam, was also a violinist and concert master in Toscanini's famed NBC Symphony Orchestra), and as it turned out, his mother, my Aunt Ethel, did know something. First big break in the case, as a detective would say.

My aunt thought that Sylvia had remarried, moved to Maryland, and her last name was now Nazdin. She also recalled that both she and Sylvia used to love little theatre groups and had acted in community theatre, so possibly she could still be doing that and serve as a way to track her down.

That was wonderful news! I had both a name and a state. In those days, way before the internet, the only way to locate someone, short of hiring a private detective (which I never thought of) was to use a phone book. So I searched all over Maryland using phonebooks, but never found any Nazdin listed.

My dad and some business partners had invested in garden rental apartment buildings in Maryland many years prior (the sale of which I discussed previously, in Chapter One). As it turned out, the woman who had been running the office there had a husband who worked for the FBI. Once I found this out, I wasted no time in asking her to inquire if he could help me find my Aunt. He found a Nazdin in Silver Spring, Maryland, but their number was unlisted, and the husband was named Leo. Leo, it turned out, according to this FBI person, likely had a job that involved the Teamsters Union. Unlisted number and Teamsters? Not a great combination for me, so I hesitated, and left this as an unfollowed lead.

When my dad passed away, I was the one responsible for selling this property and representing the three estates comprising my Dad's estate, and those of his partners. To make the situation even more complicated, it turned out that there was a ground lease on the property, in yet another estate, and I had to navigate through all of this to find a buyer. Once I had the property listed with different brokers and sources in the Laurel, Maryland area, several potential buyers emerged. One had the unusual name of Gudelsky, which was fortunate, because if the name had been Smith this story could have a different ending. Gudelsky turned out to have no interest in buying old garden apartment buildings.

Ten months later I did sell the property. YAY! I was thrilled to be done with what had taken most of my time for almost a year. I invited my daughter Debbie to go somewhere with me to celebrate the sale, and had read about a delicious sounding spa in, of all places, St. George, Utah. It felt intuitive that I was called to go there, and so we went.

Because I loved hiking so much, the big excitement for me was to go out into the red rock country and explore the scenery. The morning of our second day in St. George, I went early and met up with some other guests and felt really immersed in the hiking experience. Now when I tell you what happens next, you have to consider the odds of this happening. As I was waiting for one of the spa vans to pick me up, I overheard a woman introduce herself to another hiker. I heard her say, "Maida Gudelsky." *Hmmm*, I thought. *Where have I heard that name before?*

One of the prospective buyers for the Maryland property had that Gudelsky name, so I walked over to her and asked if she happened to be from Maryland. She said, "YES! SILVER SPRING!"

I breathlessly asked if she had ever heard of a woman named Sylvia Nazdin. She responded that she thought her mother had a friend with that name. I described how she would be in her early seventies, played the piano, had red hair, loved community theatre, loved Renoir and how I was just about flipping out with excitement to find my aunt. She agreed to ask her mother for a phone number.

The next morning at breakfast, Maida came over to me, handed me a phone number and said, "If this is the same Sylvia Nazdin, my mother thinks she will be thrilled to hear from you."

I walked in a daze back to my room. Debbie was still sleeping, and without thinking, I just picked up the room phone and dialed the number.

"Is this Sylvia Nazdin?" I asked tentatively.

"Yes" comes this glorious, theatre-honed voice.

"When I was a little girl, my name was Jo—"

I could not even finish pronouncing my name before she said, "I love you, I love you, I've loved you all your life!"

Oh my God, it was her, and we didn't stop talking for the next few hours. She told me that my dad had promised that I would never forget her, and I never did. We made arrangements for me to come to Silver Spring within the next month. Sylvia was the star at that time in a community theatre production of "Life With Father" and I was thrilled to see her perform and meet many of her friends. That felt very fitting, indeed.

I went to meet with Sylvia clutching a photo of four-year-old me and became so excited when I saw her standing in the street, also clutching a photo of herself at age 22. We hugged in the street for what seemed like an eternity—both photos were exactly how we had remembered each other. We finally made it into her house, feeling like the 50 years that had separated us had suddenly evaporated. We were united again after a half-century of never being separated in our hearts, and had another 20 wonderful years together.

You've got to believe, like I do, that Pop was looking down at that spot in the red rock country of Utah, encouraging Maida and me to somehow be in earshot of each other. I believe it was divine intervention working at its best. I had never been to Utah, never really expected to hear that name Gudelsky ever again, but how else can you explain a phenomenon like this.

Intuition and Blessings in Disguise

To me it is obvious that the more you are open to new ideas, weird ideas and trying to do things in a different way, the more likely you will be able to access your intuition. We all have it, and often when we hear that inner voice that tells us to do or not to do something, we are directly connected to our intuition.

"Rats, I should have listened to my gut, my first idea, my original thought about this," is a typical response of someone who has not followed their intuitive advice. There are always signs of whether to proceed with something or not, but if they are ignored, you are on your own to either discover something wonderful, or make a mistake.

Not all of us realize how readily accessible our intuition is, just waiting there for us to listen. Ever have a dream about something, only to have it sort of happen? That is an intuitive sign of something to come. Thoughts and dreams can portend events and ideas. It's also true that many times when we look back on something that didn't go our way, we realize that it was a blessing in disguise. The job you didn't take, or the job you didn't get, fall into this category.

When I first moved to Florida, as I waited a year just to be able to sit for a real estate license, I sold advertising for the local legal paper. The rest is history, as I describe elsewhere in this book.. How different my life would have been if I had started to sell real estate in South Florida. I probably wouldn't have written this book.

My future husband Lew moved from California to Florida one year after I did, and held a position at a company called "Leadership Housing," where I had applied for a real estate-related job. Something told me not to work there even after they offered me the job. I would have met Lew at a time when both of us were interested in other people. The Universe preferred that Lew and I meet later, and as of this writing, we have been together for more than four decades and looking back on it, I realize how lucky I was not to have taken that job. Soon thereafter, I was able to start my magazine.

Another blessing in disguise was if the magazine I applied to, *Gold Coast Pictorial*, had hired me to sell ads, there never would have been a *Broward Life Magazine*. Did they leave an opening for a great possibility for me or what? Sometimes the arbitrary decisions of others that you perceive as negative at the time turn out to be a great blessing for you, especially if you follow your intuition.

JOIE-ISM #8

If you've got a feeling about something, pay attention.
Many of the biggest mistakes we make in life come from
not listening to our own inner wisdom, our voice of intuition.

JOIE-ISM #9

Be open to receiving your own guidance.
Every answer you're ever looking for is already available within you.

JOIE-ISM #10

Attitude isn't everything, but it is almost everything.
Think young, think happy, think you can do it,
and the Universe helps you accomplish your goals.

JOIE-ISM #11

You really can't build anything without a strong foundation.
That's particularly true for character building and
the trust that good character engenders.

Joie-ism #12

Don't overthink! Just do it!
We were so deadline-oriented that sometimes overthinking
would just land us in a position of being fearful to do anything.
Employees would freeze, or say we can't do this or that,
but I always encouraged them to just go for it.
Start someplace, and like a kitten with a ball of yarn, just let it go.
See where it takes you and make it happen!

CHAPTER FOUR

All Anybody Buys Are Benefits

JOIE-ISM #13

*What makes a sale is getting someone
to see the benefits of what you have to offer.
You must educate them using their point of view and their own
needs to enable them to see the value of what you are presenting.*

Because a lot of entertainers came to South Florida to do shows at either the Hollywood Beach Hotel or the Diplomat Hotel, and in later years, at the magnificent Sunrise Theatre, we got real headliners we could feature in *Broward Life Magazine.* We started with Don Shula on the cover of the first issue, and then on subsequent covers had among other well known personalities comedian Flip Wilson, singer Olivia Newton-John, race car driver, Andy Granatelli, and golfing great Jack Nicklaus.

Our new editor, who did a lot of wonderful things for the magazine, structured the content so there were articles under sections called Featuring Life, Reviewing Life, Enjoying Life and Sporting Life. We would fit in those sections many of the local events. The first issue he edited was published January 1976, and featured a wonderful cover of Jackie Gleason, star of the TV show, "The Honeymooners." Gleason had a soft spot for us because we focused coverage on his Inverrary golf tournament so often that he happily agreed to appear on our cover along with his sidekick, the actor and comedian Art Carney.

As we were building the magazine's circulation, I was still thinking about national advertising and did have that J&B ad, so I thought I should be able to get Dewar's Scotch as an account too. After all, I even drank Dewar's. So, I looked up where their ads came from and found a nice man in New York, Scott Romer, who was in charge of their advertising. He was another guy who seemed impossible to see. When they did a liquor convention in Hollywood, Florida, I decided to buttonhole this guy to advertise in *Broward Life Magazine* and tell him I would love to be a Dewar's profile, which was their most popular advertising series.

When the event occurred I couldn't get near Romer, but I found out what room he was speaking in and I knocked on the door. He was giving a presentation to his wholesale sales staff. I told the person who answered the door, "It's very important that I see him, I need to talk with him right now, can you please get him out here."

This man, who I was never able to get on the phone when he was in New York, came to the door. I told him who I was, that I published this magazine, and I wanted very much to have a Dewar's Scotch ad. I told him we already had J&B and that he couldn't let his competitors be the only Scotch people appearing in the publication. He looked at me like I had not two heads, but three.

"What, how did you get in here?"

"Anybody can get into this liquor convention," I replied.

He started sputtering, not knowing how to react.

"It would mean so much, can you just tell me who is the man I need to talk to about becoming a Dewar's profile and getting a Dewar's ad?"

He told me the man's name, David Drake at Leo Burnett Worldwide in Chicago. I said I would contact Mr. Drake and thanked him.

Now here is where the situation got a little crazy, because a little while later, one of Romer's assistants came looking for me. I was told, "Go back, Scott Romer wants to talk to you."

I went back to the conference room and Romer said to me, "You know, would you do me a favor? I want you to come in here and address my sales people. I want you to tell them how you got to talk to me, and how I told you to get a hold of David. I wouldn't be a bit surprised if you manage to get a Dewar's ad from him. Come in and tell my sales people what you did and how you did it."

They handed me a glass of Scotch. I took a couple of sips and realized if I had much more to drink then I would not be able to tell them much of anything. I tossed the rest of the contents in a plant behind me and they took it to mean "Oh, she needs more Scotch," so they poured more and that poor plant was probably drunk by the end of the afternoon.

I had a wonderful time giving sales tips to his national sales reps and they seemed appreciative of my advice. Afterwards, I got on a plane and went straight to Chicago, had an appointment with David Drake and explained to him what I wanted. I told him how Scott Romer had sent me after my presentation to talk to his sales staff. And wouldn't you know it, we did get a Dewar's ad for our magazine.

As for the Dewar's profile, Romer said to me, "I can't believe this. We get at least 6,000 requests a year from people wanting to be a Dewar's profile. But we will help you be one."

Becoming a Dewar's Profile

Dewar's profile ads in magazines were popular beginning in the 1970s, used by Dewar's as a clever nationwide campaign to feature up-and-coming young people achieving meaningful things and who were also drinking Dewar's Scotch. My dad would have a Dewar's on the rocks everyday around five o'clock, and so when I visited him I would too. It was a special time for both of us, and I always associated drinking Dewar's with Pop, enjoying laughs together as we sipped and talked.

When being a Dewar's profile became a reality for me at the age of 34, I was just thrilled. The copy for my featured ad gave my name, home, occupation, last accomplishment, and a "why I do what I do" quote, along with a brief profile and identification of my favorite Scotch, which was Dewar's White Label.

In our November 1975 issue of the magazine, we featured the Dewar's profile of me as an ad. Many people I knew, and many more I would come to know, all saw the ad and it seemed to make quite an impression. It was an ad campaign that has survived for decades because it struck a nerve, resonating with young people like me, people who had big dreams of making a difference in the world. I was selected not only because of my persistence, but because I introduced a new magazine in South Florida. I fit their age profile, and most important of all, I really drank Dewar's!

When No Is Just a Word on the Path to Yes

The second time I went to see David Drake in Chicago, I also made an appointment in nearby Lincoln Park, to see Bill Pattis, who ran the Pattis Group. They were well known national advertising reps and at the time represented a magazine in South Florida called *Palm Beach Life*. I had this idea that I could increase my national advertisers if I could sell a combination of *Palm Beach Life* and *Broward Life* as one ad buy for the New York agencies—they had been telling me that my magazine was too small for them to advertise in. If I could do the whole coast from Palm Beach down to Fort Lauderdale, this would be a much bigger incentive for them to buy.

So I printed up a rate card, which is where you show the pricing for the different size ads. I made it a three-panel rate card and on the third panel I printed the name of the Pattis Group, their offices, who their people were, and how to contact them. I said on the rate card they were our national reps.

When I met Bill Pattis and asked him if he would be interested in being a national rep, initially he said no, pointing out how we were too small, which was the answer I expected. In response, I said, "I see that you represent *Palm Beach Life*. Why can't we do an ad buy where we sell Palm Beach and Broward together, so you can buy pretty much the whole coast? What do you think about that?"

That suggestion intrigued him. Then I said to him, "Look, I've already listed you on my rate card."

I handed him my rate card—he took one look and couldn't believe it. "You put my name on your rate card?"

"I haven't used it yet, we just printed these because I wanted to bring it to show you how natural it looks and how wonderful it would be for you to do this."

"And what would you do if I turn you down?"

I took the rate card and just ripped off the third panel containing his name. He started laughing. "Alright, let's give it a try."

It was incumbent upon me to meet with Agnes Ash, publisher of *Palm Beach Life*, to see what she thought of the idea of us having a combined advertising buy. We agreed to meet at the tony Le Club International in Fort Lauderdale for lunch. I was very careful with my diction, not wanting to sound anything like someone from New York (which wasn't too great an accent to have at that time), and I dressed in beige and even wore white gloves.

Agnes was VERY proper, and she also was the publisher of the esteemed *Palm Beach Shiny Sheet*, as well as *Palm Beach Life*, so I wanted to be as genteel and soft-spoken as possible. Our lunch was dignified and went well as we became more relaxed with each other. Once she had agreed to the value of the combined ad buy, I jumped up from the table and shouted "We will be the Kennedy & Cohen of the South Florida advertising buy!"

At the time, Kennedy & Cohen was a large appliance chain in Florida and elsewhere; they had their jingle and ads all over the place. To me it meant we would be super visible like they were. I am not sure what Ms. Ash thought, but we enjoyed each other's company for many years to come, and that ad buy idea enhanced and profited both of our magazines. Of course, she giggled, once she got to know me, that I tried to be so demure when we first met but the more exuberant me soon emerged and it was all good.

For our November 1975 magazine issue, the one in which my Dewar's ad appeared, we had J&B Scotch and Dewar's together.

It was the first time we listed having national and international representation with the Pattis Group, the most prestigious company reps at that time for advertising in magazines.

Moral of this story: Benefits make the sale. *No* is just a word on the path to getting to *yes*.

What Benefits Are in a Name?

As a little girl my family called me "Joanne." When I was six years old and had moved to Westchester County, New York and started school, one of my new friends, Marcia, decided that my name was a mouthful and didn't suit me, so she called me "Joey." That was my name all through high school and college and it wasn't until I met my first husband Michael, that I was back to "Joanne" because he preferred it. That was my name when I was teaching both as a student teacher in New York City and then in Lawrence, Long Island.

Once I moved to Florida I was still "Joanne" at work, but my friends and close associates called me "Joey." It wasn't until Bill Luening, our longtime editor at *Broward Life* changed it and I became "Joie." He changed it because he said he felt like he was sending memos to a ten-year-old boy. "J-o-i-e." I loved the spelling!

"My one affectation," I exclaimed, and so it stuck and has been my name ever since! Of course, legal documents have my long official name, but I went by Joanne Myers as my first business name in Florida.

One evening when working late at JMG Publishing, a good friend and client, George, who often showed up with a job after hours, convinced me that I should add Goodkin to my name as Lew was so well known and respected. I didn't think it was necessary, but he kept at it and finally convinced me to use my full name. For the most part I was known by either name in Florida, but once I moved to California it was just Joie.

My first minister, Dr. Tom Costa, loved to tell the story of his life when he used his birth name "Pete." In his words, nothing went well for him, and he was down on his luck and working part-time as a bartender and searching for something, but didn't know quite what. As he tells it, someone invited him to go to a Science of Mind church and it changed his life. *But his life really didn't get better until he changed his name.* Someone he met did a whole exercise using the number in the alphabet that matched the letter in his name and determined that he would never succeed as "Pete." He agreed to try using the diminutive of his middle name, and called himself "Tom." He said that changing his name changed his life. As Tom Costa he became very successful and fulfilled.

Speaking for myself, I have always been happier as Joie. I encourage you to find a nickname for yourself if you think it will have a good impact on your life. You don't have to change your name legally, but perhaps you will have more confidence or more fun if you choose your own name. See how you feel when friends use it.

I know that every sound has energy and that certain vibrations change with different letters. I have studied sound healing extensively, and will write more about that later, but want to share with you that once you agree to think outside the nine dots, or outside the box in many situations, it can bring you greater happiness and joy. You don't really need to understand it entirely. You just need to understand if there are any benefits for you.

Sometimes Benefits are ONLY in the Beholder's Eye

What about when you do everything right, but the sale still doesn't happen? When I was selling real estate in New York I encountered the most unexpected situation. There can be times where a benefit to everyone else is obvious, but if a key person necessary to making the sale sees no benefit then no sale can happen.

I was working in real estate sales for a firm in New York City and was given the assignment to find a regional headquarters for a national oil company. I combed the properties and acreage within their desired geographical parameters and found what had to be the perfect location. The others at the real estate firm agreed.

The easy part seemed to be to approach the one business on this otherwise undeveloped property, a well-loved local trattoria that had been there for many years. I thought this would be the easiest sale of my career. Name your price, a national company is interested in buying your property and the surrounding acreage. What's to think about? You surely can relocate your restaurant.

Not so fast. The owner I spoke with repeatedly said, "I live uppa stairs" and there was NOTHING I could say to entice him to either live elsewhere or work elsewhere, or even consider another location for his restaurant. The money, no matter how huge the amount, simply did not matter.

Ultimately, I had to report that the man who owned the property refused to sell. Others thought they had more experience than me, and probably thought I was just a young woman, but we have been at this for years and someone else from the office could surely persuade the buyer. No way. This guy dug in, refused any price, and simply would not sell. His priorities revolved more around preserving the quality of his marinara sauce than millions of dollars!

This story eventually illustrated two key concepts for me. One, had I closed the deal and he sold the property, I likely never would have left New York, as I would have been so established. It was another one of those be glad that you didn't make the deal or get the job situations.

Two, no matter how skilled you are in making a sales presentation, a person who sees more benefit in standing pat than in selling reinforces my belief that all anyone buys are the benefits. To this man, living "uppa stairs" and working in the same restaurant that his family had owned forever, meant more to him and had more benefit to him than buying any house or any number of houses and relocating the restaurant.

Hard for many of us to comprehend, but that was what happened. He didn't budge. I happened to look on Google maps when I was writing this story just to see what was on that property now. Guess what! A Trattoria! Yikes, I think that some son or grandson of that guy must still live "uppa stairs" and they are probably using the same marinara sauce recipe.

Making "Buying Benefits" More Worthwhile

Another bit of wisdom I learned the hard way is when something is given for free, it doesn't have value to the receiver. Think of all the junk mail and stuff we toss without looking at it. Discounted yes, free no. In my experience, for it to have value, something needs to be paid for it.

When I had a garage sale in a neighborhood not likely to have them, near the Intracoastal Waterway in Fort Lauderdale, we had gates across our driveway, and made a big deal about allowing only a certain number of people at a time to come in, after which we would close the gates. People waited patiently and as some left, the next bunch would be allowed in.

In those days I loved expensive sunglasses and had a beautiful pair that I was asking $40 for. They were likely worth several hundred. One lady kept looking at them and fondling them and trying them on, but it was obvious that even $40 would have been too much for her. After a while I said, "What would you like to pay for them?"

She replied, "I ain't got but a few dollars."

I told her they were expensive designer frames but since they looked so well on her and since she obviously liked them so much, I could lower the price, but she had to decide now. She rummaged in her purse and offered me $3. I said that would not be quite enough. I could see they were really important to her, and I did want her to have them, but I also wanted her to feel good about getting them. I said she could have them for $5. She was so thrilled that she hugged me and danced around in them.

Obviously, the value to her was great, and she was thrilled to have them. The reason I made them $5 was just that. She needed to feel that she had negotiated a great deal for herself, and I am sure I would not have sold them so cheaply had she not loved them so much. I was as happy as she was.

I have always felt wonderful providing joy to someone else. I think if those sunglasses had been free, they would not have meant nearly as much to her as they did because she had to work to get them. I sold lots of tumbler glasses too, by offering soda with each purchase. Every last tumbler glass was sold. There are always ways to create interest and excitement, even in how you structure a garage sale.

JOIE-ISM #14

Use the skills that are unique to your style and personality,
and do what is memorable.
This usually works to get you the order
or the deal or the commission.

JOIE-ISM #15

There is a fine line between being pushy and getting someone
to buy what you're selling, make the deal, see it your way,
and just be pleased with what you are offering.
It usually hangs on the hook of when you hit a nerve
that resonates with what the buyer's desires.
I know that when I spoke to the guy from J&B Scotch,
I had him when I said, "In the time you are taking to discuss
this with me, you could use some of your Christmas promotional
fund and just get the cover." He smiled at that because, yes,
he had a big budget and his time was more valuable than
gabbing with me about, as he called it, a tertiary market.

JOIE-ISM #16

If you need to sell a marketing professional on
your product or service, be sure to confirm that you are
pitching the person who has the authority to buy.
You can think you have done the greatest presentation
only to find out (or not find out) that the person who seemed so
excited about your product has to ask someone else
about purchasing it. You can get lost in the transition from the
person you pitched to, to the one who actually can buy.
Sometimes, when you cannot make an appointment
with the actual buyer, it can be helpful to ask for a date
to get back to you about it.

JOIE-ISM #17

Whenever you can, create a sense of urgency about a decision;
that helps to expedite a sale.
"We have a limited supply, and it would be
perfect for (you, your company, your customer) so can you
please let me know by Wednesday, and I will save one for you."
If it is a product that is intangible, just as my selling advertising was,
I would say, "I can hold the inside front cover for you, but I need
to know by Wednesday." Use whatever works in your situation to
create a sense of immediacy and urgency. People can let stuff slide
unless you give them a reason to provide a timely response.

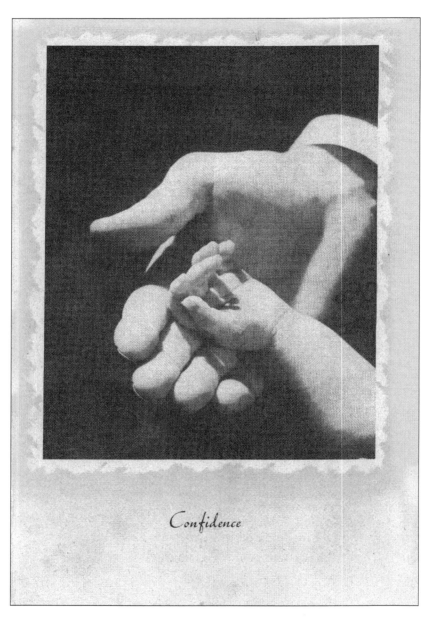

Confidence

Confidence. A theme of the book, and gift from Pop at age 5.

Silver Medallion Brotherhood Award with honorees
and Diane Sawyer, wearing the "sparkly" dress.

The Miami Herald

Introducing . . .

Friday, March 20, 1987

Joanne Goodkin, self-made publisher

> **'I** am as comfortable talking to truck drivers as I am bank presidents.'
>
> **Joanne Goodkin**

Who: Joanne Myers Goodkin, born July 7, 1941, in New York City, is owner and president of the JMG Publishing Corp. in Lauderdale-by-the-Sea.

Latest accomplishment: Directing "Hands Across Broward," getting 60,000 people to link hands along Broward beaches in October 1985 for the United Way.

Biggest Accomplishment: "Either launching Broward Life magazine from a kitchen table top . . . or creating a 23-employee publishing company, going from zero dollars a year to $1.5 million yearly in five years."

From idea to reality: "I was helping out in my husband's [real estate] office when I saw how much he was paying Sir Speedy for printing, and I said, 'For that much money, I can buy a printing press and print it for him.' So I did."

Family: Husband, real estate analyst Lewis Goodkin; and daughters Valarie, Sherrie, Debbie, and Andria. "Lew never could spell," says Goodkin. They live in Fort Lauderdale.

Education: Graduated from New York University with a bachelor's degree in English in 1963. "I changed majors about a half dozen times, then finally picked English because that was the only curriculum that didn't require any math."

Early disappointment: "After I graduated from college, I was teaching Shakespeare by dividing the class up into Montagues and Capulets and [school officials] called me down about the class getting too enthusiastic and noisy. . . . I wanted to teach the kids to love language, and they wanted me to teach them about predicate adverbs."

Later pleasures: Becoming active in South Florida community affairs, publishing Broward Life magazine from 1974 to 1981, and receiving numerous awards for volunteer work.

Secrets of success: "Asking questions. I have learned everything I know about the printing business since 1974 by gathering a group of experts and asking them as many questions as possible. I also love working with people. I am as comfortable talking to truck drivers as I am bank presidents."

Interview by Darrell Eiland. Photograph by Pete Cross.

Miami Herald profile of JMG Publishing.
Joie and Heidelberg press.

Joie at the top of Murray Peak, a frequent hike in Palm Springs, CA.

Joie and Sylvia's reunion moment captured after
50 years of searching.

DEWAR'S PROFILES

(Pronounced Do-ers "White Label")

JOANNE MYERS

HOME: Ft. Lauderdale, Florida

AGE: 34

OCCUPATION: Publisher

LAST ACCOMPLISHMENT: Successfully introduced a new city-type magazine distributed throughout the South Florida market.

QUOTE: "Our magazine is devoted to helping our readers get more out of life . . . to know how to get the most out of each day and to put that information to immediate use, is exciting for us all."

PROFILE: Vivacious, energetic and involved, she's a crime buff, art connoisseur, gourmet cook and avid reader. She saw an opportunity to fill the needs of one of America's fastest growing markets with a slick contemporary and relevant new publication.

SCOTCH: Dewar's "White Label"

Authentic. There are more than a thousand ways to blend whiskies in Scotland, but few are authentic enough for Dewar's "White Label." The quality standards established in 1846 have never varied. Into each drop go only the finest whiskies from the Highlands, the Lowlands, the Hebrides. ***Dewar's never varies.***

The original JMG press and collator,
where we went through the wall.

Patsy and Joie creating graphics at JMG Publishing.

Breaking ground to add to the building.

The building, with the completed addition to the right, "275" on top.

My custom made fancy desk with conference table.

From a tiny publication directed mainly at condo residents, Broward Life has grown into a slick, widely circulated magazine that has captured several awards, thanks to the drive of one woman — Joanne Myers.

Broward Life's Been Good For Owner-Publisher Myers

By FRED GRIMM
Herald Staff Writer

Joanne Myers first turned a profit in the publications business back in 1950 as a shrewd little red-headed eight-year-old entrepreneur renting comic books to neighborhood kids.

Twenty-eight years later, little Joanne's back in the black.

The founder-publisher-owner and oozing-with-confidence ad saleswoman for flashy *Broward Life* magazine is making money, expanding facilities and fairly bubbling with success.

She's even tempered her pursuit of the buck a bit to develop a little journalistic consciousness. "Once were a magazine can make quick money is by a special advertising section," she said, talking about a paid advertisement indistinguishable from a straight article. "It's pure gravy, but we'd never do it. We'd never sell our editorial pages."

Hardly a gross and courageous stand, but perhaps no small concession for a young businesswoman who backed into the business because it would have taken her a year to get a license to sell real estate.

THAT WAS IN 1972, after she moved to Fort Lauderdale from Scarsdale, N.Y. Except for a stint teaching high school English, it had been pure salesmanship for Joanne Myers.

She took the teaching job in 1963 after she was graduated from Syracuse University. It was what society expected of a young woman in the early '60s. There she was, gazing out over a roomful of mischievous faces. "It took me about an hour-and-a-half to decide this was not for me."

She laughed it out for a year and moved into the real estate business. "I loved it. I love calling on people . . . selling. It's a real challenge to bring two people together."

Unable to sell real estate after her move to South Florida, she tried advertising. "It was more exciting. I liked the artistic element."

In 1974, she decided there was a need for a magazine for new residents. "Everybody I talked to was from New York or Chicago or somewhere else. Nobody was a native."

INVERRARY LIFE, a tiny publication for Inverrary residents, was born in October 1974. By May, the following year, it had evolved into *Broward Life*, circulation 7,000.

It was not an instant gold mine. "I didn't sleep from May 31 to Aug. 15. We just didn't sell enough. We were carried by our printer."

Times have changed. Circulation is up to 15,000. The magazine is up to more than 80 pages and folks are paying $745 to fill one page with an ad. Myers is almost down to a five-

Turn to Page 4BR Col. 1

Joanne Myers in Broward Life Offices
. . . *'I love calling on people . . . selling'*

She Brought Magazine From Puffery to Substance

FROM PAGE 1BR

day workweek and is spending some time with her 13-year-old daughter Debbie. And the 36-year-old divorcee has finally been able to enjoy a little social life.

"My entire life had been centered around getting this magazine out of the red." She spoke while squirming self-consciously before a photographer's lens. She adjusted her hair, changed her poses and struggled not to stare at the camera. "Life is so much easier when the bottom line is black," she said.

And the magazine has evolved into something more than a profitable collection of puffery. It's a slick little magazine with graphic, striking, big-city magazine covers.

THERE ARE eye-grabbers —

buy-me covers — like the March '78 issue picturing a gorgeous young woman with pursed lips painted deep red, naked chest and neck, adorned only by a tiny silver spoon dangling from a delicate chain. "Cocaine — Should It Be Legal?" asked the teasers.

Inside, the stories aren't exactly blockbusters. They're the product of an editorial budget that's never paid more than $200 for a single freelance story.

And usually, that freelance effort is the only piece in the book that has any punch. The rest is the fluffy stuff that looks good next to slick ads touting big-ticket baubles. The focus of most of the articles is dining, dancing, dress, travel.

The freelance effort doesn't go unnoticed. This year, *Broward Life* was given three second-place awards by the Florida Magazine Association for features and commen-

tary. And it's flashy graphics took a first and second. It also picked up a certificate of merit for "general excellence."

ALTHOUGH THE newspapers in Broward County give readers far more controversy, *Broward Life* articles have not been without ripples. Editor William Luening, whom Myers hired away from the Fort Lauderdale News in the spring of 1977, has helped turn the magazine into a product a cut above the typical chamber-of-commerce, don't-rock-the-boat style magazine.

Myers, the businesswoman has developed an editorial conscience. She can point to a controversial article in last May's issue that dealt with a growing schism between Broward's old waspish east and its new ethnic west and say proudly, "That cost us $4,000 in advertising."

In October, Myers zapped The Miami Herald and other big state newspapers in her monthly column for putting money into the anti-casino gambling campaign, "not because we're in love with casino gambling, but because we felt it squandered the credibility of those news organizations."

She can relax in her artsy office now and bask in her newfound recognition. Her wall is filled with honoring plaques and photographs, including a photo of her standing with an editor of Ms. magazine.

"BUT I DON'T want to be identified with that," said the self-made woman. "I don't believe in woman's liberation. It's a crock.

"A woman isn't entitled to anything extra just because of her sex.

"Profit," she said, as the old entrepreneur crept back to the surface, "knows no sex."

Broward Life Magazine written up in the *Miami Herald*.

Anthony, Patsy, Joie and Frank
featured in *Printing Impressions* Magazine.

JMG Publishing staff featured in *Printing Impressions* Magazine.

Receiving the J.C. Penney Golden Rule Award.

President of the United Way of Broward County,
and Chairman Hands Across Broward.

Twenty-eight officials from around Broward County joined hands Friday to demonstrate support for the "Hands Across Broward" human chain.

Helping hands

Officials kick off plans for 23-mile human chain across the county

Hands Across Broward is kicked off
with all Broward cities participating.

Hands Across Broward event showing
the divers underwater holding the red ribbon.

United Way

PRESENTED TO

JOANNE MYERS GOODKIN

IN RECOGNITION OF DOING THE IMPOSSIBLE.
IT WAS SAID THAT NO ONE COULD GET FORTY THOUSAND
INDIVIDUALS ON OUR BEACHES HOLDING A RED RIBBON.
YOU NOT ONLY ACCOMPLISHED THIS, BUT YOU ADDED
AN ADDITIONAL TWENTY THOUSAND.

THANK YOU

YOUR HANDS ACROSS BROWARD COMMITTEE

JOY BEDICK	RICHARD FALLON	JOHN McCABE
ED BENTON	GARY GARRISON	DAVE MILLER
GENE BERGMAN	RALPH GOLDBERG	JORJ MORGAN
GARY BITNER	JIM HILL	RICK OTT
BRIAN BROOKS	DONNA HORWITZ	MAGDA PASCAL
ANGEL CICERONE	RON HORWITZ	ART POLLACK
SCOTT COWAN	BOB KELLEY	LAURA SEITZ
NED CRAY	ED KENNEDY	TERRY SMITH
MARY DELLAPORTA	BARBARA LANGE	GEORGE SULLIVAN
WALTER FALCK	WALTER LAUN	ROBERTA WEINSTEIN

1985

Hands Across Broward award for "Doing the Impossible"
60,000 people participated.

Crystal Tones Alchemy Singing Bowls Soundbath for friends.

Metaphysical pioneer Brugh Joy, Joie,
mandala artist Paul Heussenstamm.

CHAPTER FIVE

Always Fill a Need

JOIE-ISM #18

*Make yourself indispensable by coming up with new ways
to identify and then fill the needs of your clients.*

When I was an eighth-grade English teacher, I taught Shakespeare in a way that kids really loved. I felt they wouldn't be into this old English prose and they would think it boring, so I made it fun in ways they could connect to.

I had the kids push their desks together when I was teaching Romeo and Juliet, and let the kids climb on top of the desks and duel with yardsticks as swords, while acting out the play. By the time they had to read it, they understood the plot and the words made more sense to them. I told the kids, "You will have a much more interesting life if you read a lot, because reading opens up doors to all of life's experiences."

Administrators at the school would come rapping on my door, summon me to their office and ask, "Are you teaching pronominal adjectives? Are you teaching gerunds?" And I said, "No, I'm teaching them a love of Shakespeare."

"That isn't in your lesson plan," I was informed.

My attitude was let teachers teach where and when they see a need.

As you can imagine, I found being a teacher to be frustrating. When I saw the movie with Robin Williams, *Dead Poets Society*, I related to his style of teaching that brought so much joy to his classroom. I used to say, "If you want to write, forget about the grammar, forget about the spelling, just get your thoughts out on

69

paper. The editing comes later." That wasn't the way they wanted me to teach creative writing, but I was listening to my own inner muse about how best to be effective. Yes, there are ways to even make gerunds interesting.

Publishing was a Natural for Me

Since childhood, I've been a publisher in various ways. Most of the things I did, one way or another, involved publishing. My first publishing business when I was only eight years old involved my best friend Bebe, whose father was a cartoonist. He went into New York City every Thursday and brought back comic books he had worked on. I had this idea that if we could have our friends read them, we could charge them something, kind of like rent, and then nobody would have to buy the comic book when it came out for ten cents the following Monday.

My first venture became a comic book rental library and Bebe's father was a sweetheart about helping us. He didn't mind they were a little dog-eared when he got them back because the average comic would have been read by three or four kids.

That was the first way I filled a need for people by giving them something they wanted. We even had little library cards to record when we would collect the four or five cents we charged to read each comic book. I was excited about doing something to help my friends and I was happy to have a business and be a little entrepreneur. It was certainly a preview of what was to come for me later in life when I became a full-fledged entrepreneur.

Being Resourceful with Needs

While selling advertising in South Florida in the 1970s, something that really helped me secure bill collections, especially during the summers, was that I was fortunate to own the third car phone ever in Broward County, after the police chief and the sheriff. I don't know how I got the third phone, but I had wonderful friends at the phone company and in the sheriff's department as a result of publishing the local magazine. It was a white princess phone installed in my absolutely favorite car, a 1977 Cadillac Coupe de Ville, with plush burgundy velour seats and a sunroof that opened.

When I would go to collect from ad clients, I'd call first and say, "I'd like to come by and pick up a check today." Once a man said, "Sorry, I'm just leaving," and I replied "That's okay, I'm right outside your door." He was shocked because very few people had car phones or mobile phones in those days. He had to go inside and write me a check instead of just making excuses or avoiding me.

When people bought advertising, some had good intentions of paying typically within 30 days. Other people paid net 60 and still dragged out the payment, and some people went all the way to net 90 because you can't really take back an ad once it ran. Some people must have thought they were never going to pay the bill when they took out the ad. These people I called the net NEVERS.

That annoyed my sense of fairness and integrity. It's one thing if you have some kind of financial reversal and can't pay, or if you work out a payment schedule, or if you talk to me about keeping your word and how this can be resolved, just as I did with my magazine printer when I got into a bit of a bind. It's something else entirely if you decide you just don't want to honor your word.

One man who owed me money had a sporting goods store—in those days I was an avid tennis player—and I said to him, "Look, you owe me this money and you've had enough time to pay it. It appears you just refuse to pay it, so I would like to take these tennis outfits and we'll just trade for it. How would that be?" The man was embarrassed because he knew he owed me the money, so I ended up taking the tennis outfits in exchange for his debt.

This was just one of many times when I had to take merchandise in trade because somebody was a net NEVER. These types forced me to be resourceful in meeting my bill collection needs when my own survival was at stake.

Being True to Your Word Builds Friendships

Just as it ultimately is best to surround yourself with the best people to do the job, you may not be the person in the position to do so. Sometimes we don't initially recognize the great potential of someone who might seem on the periphery of our work.

When *Broward Life Magazine* first had a "real office" in an office building, the night janitorial crew often arrived before I left. This was in the mid 1970s and I became friendly with the head of the family crew, Raymond. Ray, to this day is a dear friend and the kind of man that if you can count friends like this on one hand in your lifetime, you are very lucky.

From those earliest days, as we got to know each other, we developed a mutual respect. Ray also worked at a bank for a period of time, and I remember they had considered him for a position dealing with minority funding. He wasn't particularly comfortable with this, and had lots of concerns about such a job. I suggested questions for him to ask the bankers so he could better determine whether or not he wanted to be considered for the position. We had conversations about all sorts of things, and soon Ray was helping me with tasks at home, and helping the magazine with whatever was needed.

By the time JMG Publishing started, Ray was the obvious person to do our deliveries. He was always willing to do anything that he could to be helpful, and he soon became indispensable. As JMG grew and the deliveries increased, we realized we were really wearing out Ray's van. He never asked for help with repairs and was always there with a ready smile. By the time we moved to our own office building, Ray's van was on its last legs. To surprise him, I sent him to the dealer that had sold him his vehicle and told him I could help with repairs. Then I alerted the dealer's sales manager. Instead of the cost of the repairs, he told Ray that he could pick out any van and drive it off the lot! "Choose any options you want!"

Ray was flabbergasted, and for me it was a great moment to help a friend who had been so loyal for so many years. He was reluctant to accept the new van, but I convinced him that he had earned it and he hadn't signed up to get his van wrecked by helping with our ever-growing deliveries.

We bonded as friends for life and still talk on the phone and celebrate holidays and birthdays. He still lives in the same family home he had when I was in Florida. Who would have thought that our mutual kindness would mean so much to both of us.

I encourage you to see people around you with new, bigger eyes than you think the person warrants. We don't often realize how we have many prospective friendships around us just waiting to be developed. There is no one I could count on to do all of the things Ray did so graciously to help us. Treat people as you would like to be treated, get to know them slowly, and see what potential friends may have been placed in front of you. None of us realizes everything about co-workers and casual acquaintances but by spending time with them—converse about all sorts of things and you may just make a life-long friend! Keep your mind open as our preconceived notions often don't turn out to be true.

Caring so much about people keeping their word was the basic value Ray and I shared, and the basis of building our friendship. If Ray said he would do something, I never thought about it again. I knew it would be done. What a luxury that trust is when you are running a stressful deadline-driven business. Define your values and know what you want. Give this some real thought and view others based on their character and your experience with them keeping their word.

Seeing a Need for a New Printing Company

When I sold *Broward Life Magazine*, I felt like a fish out of water. Just for something to do, I went to work in my husband's office at Goodkin Research filing invoices. One of the invoices I filed was from a printing company charging my husband what I thought was an exorbitant amount to print his real estate research reports. Their prices were nuts! So much so, that I thought maybe it would be a good idea to get our own printing press and do it all ourselves.

"For that kind of money, we should own a press!" I told Lew, not knowing for a second that I was making a prophetic statement.

I called the printer and asked what kind of press they used to print the Goodkin reports, which were always in blue ink instead of black. They told me they used an A.B. Dick and a Multi. Neither words meant anything to me, though perhaps I had heard somewhere about A.B. Dick copying machines.

Out of curiosity, I called A.B. Dick in Miami and asked, "Do you have a press that prints in blue ink?"

"Lady, we got a press that can print any color you want."

I inquired whether I could speak with someone about a small press that our office might use to print research reports in blue ink. Had this been any other time, the guy might have blown me off, but we were in a recession, interest rates were 20 percent and nobody was buying equipment unless they absolutely had to. The A.B. Dick guy ended up coming to our office with a colorful brochure showing a woman in red high heels standing in front of this printing press that could meet our needs.

"Hey, it can't be that complicated if a woman in high heels can operate it, right!" *Wrong, wrong, wrong!*

We had it delivered to our supply room and it came with all sorts of chemicals and ink and rags and assorted cleaning bottle jars and brushes. It was a printing press and it had a much higher learning curve than the colorful brochure indicated. High heels, indeed!

Craig, from A.B. Dick, had made it seem like a glorified Xerox machine, as if it wouldn't take much more than a secretary to run it. But after we bought it, suddenly Craig was always being called to come to our office and run the press, and the secretary who was asked to help would come in wearing battle fatigue outfits and camouflage. She would be in there tinkering with this press for hours, moaning and looking distraught, almost in tears. She was a very capable person, but dealing with that press was total frustration for her.

Craig realized he had presented the press to us in an oversimplified way and felt an obligation to make sure we could eventually run the press ourselves. But we really had no one qualified to learn how to operate it. We needed someone who really knew what they were doing, so I asked Craig if he knew anyone who could run the press part-time. He took me to meet Tony, who worked for another printer.

In those days Tony was making $5 an hour, so I offered him $6 an hour, which in 1980 was a typical wage for this type of work. He started printing Goodkin Research reports on our own press. They were spiral bound, had special covers, and the finished product was impressive, though it was difficult to put them together in that small supply room space at our offices. These bound reports were the market and feasibility studies that Goodkin Research did for major developers and financial institutions.

To the rescue came our salesman Craig once again. "I think you guys need a collator."

"A what?" I asked.

"A collator that can attach to this machine and it will automatically collate the pages and then you just have to bind them. There obviously is no room in here, but is there someplace else you can set this up?"

"Uh, sorry, no."

By then the pinstriped employees of my husband's firm were not thrilled with stepping over boxes of paper and smelling all sorts of chemicals either. I had the bright idea to ask the guy next door if I could go through our adjoining wall and rent some space from him. He thought I was totally nuts, but when I didn't see any other place to put this collator thing, I went back and explained to the guy that we could open the wall and enclose some of his space, and I would of course, pay him generously for allowing this sublet to us. After many conversations and overcoming enumerable objections, we went through the wall and the collator had a new home.

At this point I thought I needed a corporation to own all this equipment, and I gave absolutely no thought to what to call it. JMG Publishing Corporation, which were simply my initials, was the first name that popped into my mind. Okay! I have a corporation, now I own a press and a collator, and Tony is happy to come several evenings a week.

As JMG Publishing started to become a real printing business, I realized we needed our own stationery and logo. I asked my friend Greg for his graphics design firm to do that, and he assigned one of his designers, Patsy, who did an awesome job. She made the initials of JMG look like a large roll of paper in our printing process. I loved the colors (teal, ivory and burgundy) and the total design.

It seemed that the best way to amortize our equipment was to see if any other people in the building needed some printing. I knocked on the door across the hall and asked, "We just got a press for our reports, do you need any printing done that we can do on it?" Initially the man said no, but within a month he gave us a try. Not shy about asking other tenants in the building, we were soon quite busy.

At its highest point, JMG Publishing had 30 employees and we ran the presses 16 hours a day. As we grew, our available space shrank even more. It was getting pretty wild having a printing business in the middle of an upscale consulting business. Work boots and wingtips didn't coalesce easily. The employees and clients trying to navigate into their conference rooms had to pass piles of stacked paper, jars of unknown mystery, and all sorts of rags and bags.

Growing the business wasn't that difficult, as the key to doing that, as in any business, is identifying and then filling a need. The tenants in our office building were happy to just walk down the hall or take the elevator a couple of floors, and voila! there was a place to get their printing done quickly.

I think there were also two other reasons why we grew so rapidly. One was that political printing had to be paid for at the time it was picked up. As the former publisher of *Broward Life Magazine*, I knew almost all the politicians in Broward County. I let them know that I wanted to do their printing and would get it back to them fast. That helped to fill the coffers quickly, and I was able to rehire Brenda, my former assistant from *Broward Life*.

Two Business Dynamos Joined Forces

In November1981, the *Fort Lauderdale News* and *Sun Sentinel* magazine asked me, "What are you doing now that you sold *Broward Life*?" Based on my answer, they wrote an article about me and my husband Lew, and positioned it as "Two business dynamos join forces to achieve personal happiness."

In that article, I was questioned about my growing printing business, which up until that point, was a type of quick printing operation, and I blurted out, "We want to specialize in doing annual reports," and other collateral brochures, as I thought that would be a good way to expand and attract business. I was still very active in the community, and to illustrate that another headline in the story was "Publisher Joanne Myers: Crime Stoppers is her Latest Crusade."

After the article came out, I told Greg, who was a partner in a very skilled graphic design firm, that I would love to do annual reports and collateral brochures. He and his associates had done some great graphics, photography and artwork for my magazine. I told him if I can sell these, I can job out the design work to his firm. We shook hands on that, and shortly thereafter I landed my first annual report job.

My husband already knew Dennis, head of the International Union of Operating Engineers local. They needed to do an annual report, had read the newspaper article about my printing business, and had asked me to attend a board meeting to present what my firm could offer. Greg came to the meeting with me. It was comedic, like something on Saturday Night Live.

Somber-faced people were seated around a large boardroom conference table, all men except for one very demure, petite, 90-pound woman with long curly hair and huge glasses. She turned out to be their attorney, and the only words she repeatedly uttered were "not prudent."

I liked Dennis, but he was a very forceful, volatile man, and pounded his shoe on the table whenever he wanted to disagree with the previous person. Greg seemed nervous and uncomfortable, but

I was winging a sales pitch in uncharted waters, and offered them a complete annual report with editing services if needed. "Soup to nuts," the whole works in full color and I don't remember the quantity, but I threw out a budget of $30,000. That seemed like it would cover whatever we wanted to do, and after two more meetings we managed to nail down the job.

All progressed well. Greg's firm did an awesome job, and I farmed out the actual printing to the firm in Miami that had previously printed my magazine. Our client was thrilled—we had done our first annual report, but then a big glitch surfaced. The job was actually $19,000 not $30,000, so I approached Dennis and asked him what he wanted us to do.

Integrity is essential in business, and it will come back to you many times over if you are honest and truthful with clients about anything that does not go quite according to plan. Dennis felt that the budget had been approved for printing, and was willing to use up the balance in printing jobs in the future. It took some time and insistence that we use a union typesetter, but he was my first big printing client.

At that point I felt confident enough to approach my colleagues on various civic boards about doing their printing. One man, who turned out to be a dear friend, blurted out, "You want to do my what?"

"Printing, you know, envelopes, letterhead, brochures, whatever," and he looked at me like he couldn't believe it. Fancy me in my high heels and silk blouses and pearls wanting to do his printing! He referred me to his purchasing agent, and we got a job to print 20,000 two-color #10 envelopes. Great!

I was all excited until I told Tony. He responded, "We can't do that on this press. The registration has to be exact (the two colors have to line up perfectly) and it needs a two-color press to do it."

We did try to run it through twice on our press and it was a disaster. So, once again, I jobbed it out to someone else, but I knew we had to expand so I would soon have room for a two-color press.

Our Expansion Brings Us Even More Business

One day Greg's graphic designer, Patsy, approached me about wanting a reference from me, as she was looking for another job.

"Why don't you work for me?" I asked.

"Doing what?"

"What would you like to do?"

She thought about that and replied, "I'd like to work on annual reports."

"Okay, I'll go get one."

Many years later, while I was writing this book, Patsy admitted to me: "You said that to me like getting an annual report contract was as easy as going to Publix to pick up a dozen eggs. I thought I had landed in The Twilight Zone. But you came back with the annual report, just like that."

My impetus for going full speed after the annual report business was likely Patsy's desire and creative ability to work on them. Think big we did, and as a result, we continued growing and didn't look back. Patsy too got squeezed into the Goodkin office space and we officially had ourselves a great graphic designer. Our logo tagline was "Designers, Printers and Publishers," and so we were!

We were bursting at the seams of our office space and were definitely wearing out our welcome at Goodkin Research. We had squeezed into corners of other people's offices and needed to move—the chemical smells alone would have tossed us out of anywhere else. Our bindery space was the size of a small kitchen counter, and Brenda and I affectionately called ourselves "The Laverne and Shirley Bindery."

Lew and I made the decision to look for more office space that we could rent or purchase, to house our two businesses. A building on Commercial Boulevard in Lauderdale by the Sea seemed perfect, and happened to be for sale. Paine Webber occupied the entire top floor, leaving 5000 square feet for us to share. Seemed like we would never outgrow that! But JMG continued to encroach on Goodkin Research space as our business grew by leaps and bounds, and soon the growing prepress department and camera department left us with less space for our designers and two presses.

JMG's growth and our ability to design so many complicated jobs couldn't have occurred without Frank. He had supreme skills and was one of the best prepress and printing guys in all of South Florida. So often he would say to me, "We can't do that!" And I would say back, "We have to, I just sold it."

You could hear him sighing and muttering, but he always found a way to do it. He was so skilled and knew the equipment that other printing companies had, as many were his clients too. Our deal was that he had space in our building and could run his own business, so long as he gave our work priority.

We were able to give him tons of challenging work, and his skills enabled us to say yes and compete to produce any job, no matter how complex. Without him we could not have jobbed out so much work to other printers in Miami. He was key to our unique success within the industry.

As luck or fate would have it, the lot next to our building was vacant and for sale. *Hmmmm? If I added on to our building, we would have enough space for more presses and an expanded art department for our graphic designers. My office could also be large enough to accommodate a conference table.*

Never having thought in terms of building, I suddenly found myself with the prospect of buying land, and yes, adding to our building and creating a fabulous printing plant and bindery. The lot was narrow and most people would have thought it wouldn't work, but by building on it we could add 5,000 square feet to our facilities. It would have to be two stories with a freight elevator at the back of the building. The back street was not going to interfere with Paine Webber or other tenants, so why not? We purchased the property and my favorite bank, known then as NCNB, financed it.

It was the beginning of the wild 80's in South Florida and everything seemed to be booming. I found a wonderful contractor and his engineer designed the plans to our specifications. It was an exciting project for them too, as they had never constructed a printing plant before. The electrical needs alone made it a great learning experience for the entire team, especially me.

We held a memorable groundbreaking ceremony with a ribbon and shovels turning the earth, and my key employees and I were excited to be growing the business again. As the earth moved, literally, we were inspired to sell more, do more, produce more and generally felt that we were going to succeed at building a great plant and bindery. Attitude can be everything, and at that time, everyone was excited and delighted to be planning and suggesting stuff that we would like. A team effort is best, and once the ideas are out there, it is up to whomever is in charge to whittle it down to the best of them. We were definitely impacted by the restrictions of the building code and other regulations for what we wanted to do, but overall, it was an exciting project that generated much enthusiasm . . . .

Clomp! Clomp! Clomp! As I would make my way across the shiny painted concrete floor of the new pressroom in my high heels about which a newspaper writer said "some reptile had to die for," I often wondered how the guys always seemed to know when I was coming to check on something.

"Are you kidding! We can hear you from the elevator," they confessed. I don't know how or why, but my energy would often cause one of the presses to "roll up," meaning it would stop working properly in my presence.

"Stay back," our pressroom manager Tony would often yell at me, because he knew my getting closer to the machine could cause it problems. The joke around the company was my energy was so high and so intense that I could stop a press!

These truly were heady, high-energy days.

A "Stylish" Example of Buying "Benefits"

Great clothes, especially shoes and handbags, were always fun for me, one reason being because I thought dressing myself was not unlike painting on a canvas. Colors and accessories always mattered and I loved odd color combinations. I was often told, and continue to be told to this day, that I looked "so put together."

One of my best business buddies, George, who helped so much with our Hands Across Broward event, and who headed Florida Power & Light, gave Lew and me two expensive tickets to a formal charity ball, something we typically wouldn't attend. I didn't have an appropriate dress and it seemed crazy to go out and buy an expensive gown that would be worn for only one or possibly two occasions. It just didn't matter to me to have something particularly fancy.

My first bright idea was to head to the consignment shop that was always so willing to resell some of my own clothing. Once there, I looked on the racks and there really was nothing suitable for this event. As I was leaving the shop, I spotted a basket in the far corner by the front window, and there, curled up, was a pleated lovely shade of peach fabric. I picked it up like a drowned puppy and was surprised to see that it was a one-shoulder gown by the designer, Mary McFadden, who was then famous for tight pleats.

Oh, I need to try this on! It was way too large for me, but I loved the design, as the one shoulder had all of these rose and pink jewels that created the back where it connected to the rest of the mostly backless dress. Wow! I headed for the dressing room after being told there was a tailor a few doors away who could fix it before the evening event.

I was greeted by the tailor who said, as he slapped his hand to his forehead, "Not that dress again! I can't work on that fabric and I wish they would stop sending customers over here!"

Needless to say, I was disappointed and went back to the consignment store. They were selling the dress for $80, whereas if brand new it would likely have been several thousand dollars. It just didn't seem to fit anyone. They offered it to me for $60, and I told them it wasn't the price. The problem was if I can't wear it that night, I didn't want or need it. "If I can get a seamstress to fix it today, I will buy it, but let me ask her first."

I was a known donor of clothing to this store, so they let me take the dress with me. I called this wonderful seamstress who worked at Saks Fifth Avenue. She wasn't in that day but I badgered and asked for her home number, until they finally relented and gave it to me (once again, persistence pays). I called her and she said she was home visiting family, but I could come over and she would see if it would be possible to fix. I rushed and arrived breathlessly to show her this wonderful dress. She chuckled and mumbled that it couldn't be fixed properly in time to wear that evening, however she could try to baste it up and fix it temporarily just so I could wear it that night.

Back at the store they saw me and quickly bargained, oh you can have it for $45, but before I could finish telling them that I found a seamstress willing to do a makeshift quickie job, just so it would survive the night on me, the sales woman said, "Please take it, you can have it for $25."

The seamstress then called around 5 p.m. and said she would have to sew it on me to make it work. So I went to her house wearing nothing but underwear and a raincoat. *Voila!* Just like Cinderella I was ready to go to the ball, though I had to sit very carefully in the car so nothing snapped or ripped.

As we arrived at the gala, flash bulbs popped like at a Hollywood premiere. We were seated at a table with people where one wife was bragging she had spent $6,000 for the Bob Mackie gown she had on that evening. *Yikes*, my first thought, social activist that I was, *how many hungry people could you feed with a dress costing that much?* It really didn't sit well with me so I blurted out that I had found the dress I was wearing at the last minute at a consignment shop. "And guess what? I only paid $25 for it!"

You should have seen their faces. It may have smelled a little musty, but that lady turned almost the same shade of green as her pricey Bob Mackie gown.

The lady who purchased the $6,000 gown must have thought there was some benefit for her to proclaim its expense, touting Bob Mackie, a top designer at the time, whereas I found more of a benefit from finding a consignment-shop gown that was just as stylish— but cost me only $25, a fraction of hers.

People admired my dress all night long, and the wildest turn of events occurred the next day, when my photograph was featured, wearing that gown, on the society page of the local newspaper. I think it's a great illustration of pretentious stuff meaning truly nothing, and the real value of something is in the eyes of the beholder.

Learn to Think Economically, Not EGO-nomically!

If you are going to start a business without a lot of funding, or even if you have unlimited funding, here are my thoughts on the best way to begin. I have taught many to think of their business as the center of an archery target. Focus, focus, focus on what you need to accomplish first, in order to progress to the second phase.

If you let things grow naturally, you will be able to correct mistakes and rethink some of your methodology and procedures. Think economically not EGO-nomically! Expand to the outer rings of that target in a natural progression. Spend as you need to and try to work with as few others as you need. Multitasking is a great plus when you are just starting out. Today the internet offers all kinds of services, from mailing and fulfillment to websites. You don't want to have any more overhead than is absolutely necessary.

My businesses grew from scratch because there wasn't ever a thought of needing an especially nice reception area, or a fish tank that required maintenance. Focus on your product or service and grow your sales so that you create a cash flow that meets your needs. If you go into debt, you just make it that much harder to get ahead. Of course, there are lines of credit, and I used them too, but be very mindful to minimize borrowing.

There are always creative ways to think about how to accomplish something and resources that you might never consider for needed items. But keep an open mind and if you can get advice and ask questions of people who know more than you, or have the experience you need, then by all means, let them help you.

When *Broward Life Magazine* moved into its first office, I found my desk by scouting the alley behind the building and being surprised that someone had actually abandoned a large desk out there. I had help taking the drawers out to make it lighter to move, bringing it up to our office and standing it in the elevator. Once it was upstairs, I created a great look for it that resembled marble by using paint and sticky paper. Then I invested in a glass top. I had a beautiful executive desk with little investment.

Ultimately, my last office at JMG was about 500 square feet with a beautiful white leather couch, oversized, matching side chairs, gorgeous tables and artwork. That office with its custom-made desk, was included in a newspaper feature called "Rooms At The Top." A photo of that desk with its attached round conference table is included, as it was just too awesome not to show you.

So always keep in mind that if you stay focused and aren't afraid to ask for help, you will be much more likely to reach and even outperform your desired goals.

JOIE-ISM #19

Find a need and fill it.
If you do something that benefits other people,
this will become the reason they will buy your product or service.
If it makes their life easier in any way, or amuses them,
that's how you can grow your business.

JOIE-ISM #20

*It's really important, whatever you're doing,
to keep your word. That defines who you are.*
That's your character. No matter what kind
of business you have, you do yourself an enormous injustice
by not keeping your word, because it colors every impression
that the person you are dealing with will have of you.
Treat people like you would like to be treated.

JOIE-ISM #21

You must do a lot of work behind the scenes
to make something look effortless.
A great slogan is a distillation
of a great many words.

JOIE-ISM #22

Someone coaching you can't do it for you.
They can be excited about your project and give you great advice,
but if you don't do it, well then,
it ain't gonna happen.

CHAPTER SIX

Put Yourself in Another's Shoes

JOIE-ISM #23

See the other person's perspective.
Learn to speak their lingo and understand
what it is they want to hear, so you can adjust what you
have to offer them based on their needs.

*She [Joie] is as comfortable talking to truck drivers
as she is to bank presidents.*

— FROM A *MIAMI HERALD* PROFILE

An opportunity can present itself out of nowhere when you least expect it that changes your life or the life of someone else. One such incident occurred for someone when I was aimlessly walking into Raley's, a local supermarket. I noticed a sign about kids raising money to go to camp. Standing stoically nearby was a kid, about eleven. He had a canvas duffle bag with all sorts of stuff in it to sell to raise money to attend camp. I think the average price was eight dollars and he had a canteen, a fanny pack, and a bunch of stuff that had no particular salability. It was just stuff to try and raise funds from the people going in and out of the store.

I watched him, noticing that as no passersby stopped, he tended to scowl and recede into almost hiding behind the duffle bag. I walked over to him and said, "My name is Joie, what's yours?"

He shyly answered "Miguel."

"I bet you think all these people aren't stopping because they're not interested in you or what you're offering." He looked at me quizzically, and I continued, "You know Miguel, these people are thinking about asparagus and dinner and a million other things. I bet most of them just walk right by without even really seeing you at all."

He seemed surprised. I explained that most people just head into the store and never notice anything unusual, such as him selling stuff. He seemed confused, so I said, "Miguel, it is NOT PERSONAL that they don't see you, or even if they do, if they don't choose to buy something. They are not giving you any thought. If they look at your stuff, it could be that they just don't need it, don't want it, or don't even want to take the time to look at it. IT'S NOT ABOUT YOU. There may be other times in your life when you're trying to sell something, and you'll have to realize the prospect is not rejecting you. I've sold a lot of stuff in my life and believe me, people are not rejecting the seller personally; they just may have no need for your product, or no time or interest to look at it. Please, Miguel, do the best you can to sell this stuff, but realize that it isn't about rejecting you."

I did buy something so he could make a sale, and then I said goodbye and headed back to my car. Behind me I heard him shout, "Miss Joie, Miss Joie," and I turned around to see Miguel heading towards me. With outstretched arms he grabbed me around my waist and said, "I will never forget you Miss Joie."

WOW! Now it was my turn to be stunned, but Miguel was serious and held on to me. When we looked into each other's eyes, he said, "You made a big change in my life today," and I knew what he was telling me was true.

That simple interaction with a stranger, to make a kid feel better about himself, was the best use of my time in those few minutes we shared together. How often do we fail to realize the positive impact we can have on a complete stranger, which costs us nothing but a little caring and a small bit of our time?

Show Curiosity About Other People

Since childhood I've had a fascination with organized crime. There was something about those guys being their own law and a whole universe unto themselves that I found totally amazing.

When I was living in Westchester County, New York, I met a man on a tennis court named Carl, whose last name had been a prominent one in organized crime parlance. I happened to mention to him that I was intrigued with organized crime. He asked me some questions and seemed absolutely shocked that I knew the subject so well. I must have sounded like a quiz show contestant.

He said to me, "I'm going into the city, I'll take you with me. I'm going to meet someone whose name is very prominent in the newspapers for being associated with organized crime, but I'm not going to use your real name because I don't want him to know who you are."

We drove into the city and my friend Carl kept calling me Bernice, which felt kind of weird. We went to a restaurant in Little Italy and met Joe Columbo, and his girlfriend, Edith. At the time Mr. Columbo was an alleged Mafia boss but he was also involved with a real estate company and we talked a little bit about real estate and Carl talked about opera.

Not long afterward, when I was back in Westchester County, I left my car in front of Carl's house after a tennis game. I came back to find that someone had deflated all of the tires. Carl told me, "I don't want them to know who you are, so don't come by my house anymore."

I realized that however fascinated I might have been by their stories, Mafia types were not anybody I really wanted to get to know. When Joe Columbo was shot but survived an assassination attempt a few years later at an Italian Day rally on Columbus Circle, I thought: *My God, that is the person who I spent time with.* That was as close as I ever got to a real Mafioso type and as close as I ever again wanted to get.

Years after meeting Columbo, while publishing *Broward Life Magazine*, we ran an article about how organized crime had moved into South Florida. We accompanied the article with this fabulous magazine cover picturing an iron bed on the beach, with a character dressed up as a stereotypical mobster, wearing a fedora, black suit, white tie, and carrying a violin case.

Soon after the article appeared, a group called the Italian American Civil Rights League showed up at our office. They were three burly guys who came in around lunchtime when no one was at the reception desk. I walked out and they said, "We're here to see the boss."

They looked a little intimidating, so I said, "The boss isn't here right now, so please take a seat."

Then I ran in and asked our editor to please call the sheriff's department and tell them to send someone over. When I knew someone with the sheriff's office had arrived downstairs, I went out and said to these guys, "I have to tell you that I am the boss."

They didn't believe me. "No, we'll wait for him." They just assumed it had to be a man.

So I told them, "Open up the magazine and look in the front; see what it says the name of the publisher is, see the picture, it's a woman. She looks familiar right? She's a redhead. It's me. I'm the boss."

I ushered these three guys into my office and tried to put myself in their shoes by explaining how sometimes people will write things that could feel like a sunburn, it kind of prickles the skin, it's annoying, it hurts, but the only recourse with a publication is to write a letter to the editor. "Because we're not going to print a retraction. This is what we found to be the truth."

They thought our article was very unfair to Italians. I said to them, "Please write a letter to the editor and I promise you we will publish it, whatever it says." That's where we left it and that's what they did. They didn't bother us again after we gave them an outlet for expressing what was on their minds.

We were also lambasting all kinds of politicians in the magazine, as our editor W.D. Luening (Bill to his friends, Willie Willie to me) had been the hard-hitting political writer for the *Fort Lauderdale News*. I talk more about Bill elsewhere in this book, but he is the one who changed the magazine's focus to more substance and journalistic integrity that we came to be known for. It was very fortunate for me that in my office I had a false door. It was in a wall and I had it covered with a full-length poster of Elvis Presley, all dressed up in one of his fabulously bejeweled outfits. When my assistant would signal me that somebody was in our office who I might not want to see, I would just walk through the Elvis door. They would look in my office and not find me there. That happened a few times.

The point was we had to keep our integrity and that carried over in everything we wrote and did. That's what journalism really is and it's what is needed for people to stand up for what is right, to tell their truth and let the chips fall where they may. By doing this we had a very successful publication. People found it interesting and hard-hitting, not just public relations fluff.

Don't Take Advantage of People

Putting yourself in someone else's shoes means understanding when they are uninformed, or vulnerable, or deserving of a break in life, and it means not taking advantage of them, even when the circumstances might benefit you.

To illustrate what I mean, when I sold my Jaguar, I put an ad in the local paper. A man answered the ad who worked as the new butler for Walter Annenberg, owner of *TV Guide* and many other publications, and who had a 220-acre estate near Palm Springs. The butler was an absolutely stunning, tall, lean Englishman with silver gray hair who had just recently arrived in the U.S. Annenberg had told this gentleman that his junker car could not be parked in the estate's driveway and he must purchase a much nicer car.

The butler said, "I like your car, I'll take it."

I answered, "Let me give you some advice. When you are in America and you buy something used, don't say you'll take it. You have to look at it, you have to kick the tires, you have to test drive it, notice the scratches. You have to make me an offer. Don't just say you'll take it or you'll get taken advantage of."

So the butler drove my car, he opened up the trunk and decided his luggage would fit in the trunk, and then said, "Okay, I don't mind paying the full price."

"Are you buying the car, or is Mr. Annenberg buying the car?"

He said he was buying the car, so I told him, "Then you shouldn't pay full price. Anybody who's selling something used is expecting you to negotiate with them. Just make me an offer."

"What kind of offer should I make?"

I replied, "Let's take off $500." I was negotiating against myself at that point. He said okay. I showed him the car had a Florida license plate and it was going to cost $300 to re-register it in California so he had to put that into the equation too. He was so grateful that I had been so fair and accommodating with him.

That is just an example of a typical person I would make a deal with. I would have normally loved to fight someone tooth and nail over a great price, but I couldn't do that with him because it wasn't a level playing field. He was new to this country and didn't know any better—it just would have been wrong to take advantage of him.

Learn How to Defuse Controversy

Being the president of the board of the United Way meant I was in charge of leading the meetings. Early in my tenure, the agenda for the meeting was to decide which new agencies seeking funding would be allowed to make a presentation to the board. It should have been a fairly simple vote to just name them and ask for raised hands to signal a yes or no vote. This meeting got off to a good start, but when the agency requiring the vote was Planned Parenthood, there was dissension and vociferous comments.

Even when I explained how this vote was only about allowing them to make a presentation and not about approving them as a new agency, it didn't seem to matter. One of our new board members, recently sent to Fort Lauderdale as the person in charge of the Tribune Company, owner of the local *Fort Lauderdale News-Sun Sentinel* newspapers, objected to their presentation based on some of their positions. As the president it was up to me to maintain order and keep the meeting moving along, so I suggested that we table that vote and move on to the next agency that was applying for funding.

This new board member was an affable, imposing man who looked every bit the executive who was used to making decisions and having his wishes respected. I thought about how to approach him, and finally chose to invite him to lunch. I knew I would have to be prepared for a continuation of his opposition at the next United Way board meeting, so I did a little background research on his home city of Chicago's relationship to Planned Parenthood thinking that maybe I could learn something that might influence him. Fortunately, my love of reading had introduced me to Albert Lasker, who did many great civic things in Chicago. He is the man credited with creating print advertising, calling it "salesmanship in print" and was the first to create print ads.

Once we were at lunch, I was careful not to immediately bring up our situation. I thought it would be fun to talk about his favorite sports team, the Chicago Cubs. At that time, the Cubs were owned by the Tribune Company. That got him relaxed and we had a pleasant lunch. As we neared the end of our time together, I casually mentioned Albert Lasker was the man who named Wrigley Field, and he was also one of the early Cubs' owners with the Wrigley brothers. He knew about Albert Lasker and the Cubs. I ventured forth using my research. "Do you know that Albert Lasker also was the one to give early funding to Margaret Sanger for her clinic?" No, he didn't know that. Margaret Sanger's clinic became Planned Parenthood.

"Now, as a devoted Cubs fan, in memory of dear old Albert, can you see your way to skip the next board meeting? I will put you down as a 'no' when we vote on this, and you don't need to be upset by our having to take this vote. Let's toast Albert Lasker and the many great contributions he made to Chicago." That approach did get a smile from him, and he agreed to skip the meeting.

Wow! I wobbled on my high heels out of that lunch, almost needing to hold on to something. Ultimately, the vote passed for Planned Parenthood to make a presentation to our board, and my lunch companion and I became co-workers on many other civic projects and shared an easy relationship with mutual respect for one another over many years.

Use as a Role Model Someone Who Relates to Everyone

Many years ago there was a fabulous *New Yorker* magazine cover of a map showing New York, the Hudson River, and then Cleveland and Peru, and nothing beyond. That's how I remember thinking of New York, as the center of the universe.

When I was growing up I just thought everybody elsewhere had the theaters and variety of restaurants and museums like we did in New York. But as I got older, I realized, my God, we were so blessed growing up so close to New York City with all of its fabulous cultural treasures, particularly the magnificent 42nd Street library where my dad took me many a Saturday.

To me the best newspaper was *The New York Times,* and to this day I find it to be informative and well written and it's the only paper, no matter where I am, I will try to read every day. I think that comes from my experiences as a little kid being around my dad's dear friend, Nat Goldstein, who was everybody's dear friend in New York. Nat started at *The New York Times* in 1924 as a copy boy, and rose to become the worldwide circulation director. The way Nat became my uncle was he lived in our apartment building and spent a lot of time with us when I was a young child, so much so that he became a part of our family.

He would come over and sit at our kitchen table with Dad and another man who had an unusual name, Turner Catledge. Later in life I found out Mr. Catledge became the managing editor of *The*

Times. I was three years old and would crawl under the table and tie and untie the men's shoelaces, once even tying one man's laces to the other man's shoes.

Nat was a delightful man, everyone loved him. When you would meet him, he would always offer you some little trinket. I remember a little pocketknife he gave me that said *The New York Times* on it. Nat once had an audience with Pope Pius XII and the first thing he asked him was, "Your Holiness, are you getting your *New York Times* on time?"

I realize now he had a much bigger influence on my life than I ever knew. I was so proud of his association with the newspaper and what it represented. He was there almost 50 years and was credited with building the worldwide circulation. Memories of Nat make me realize what an important role publishing has played in my life, ever since I was a little girl, when my love of libraries, my love of publishing, print publications and my budding entrepreneurial spirit as a businesswoman all began.

One night my first husband and I went to Sardi's restaurant for dinner. It was a world-famous eatery in New York, catering to the Broadway crowd. Theatre patrons and actors would go there, and it was then located right next door to *The New York Times* headquarters when my uncle was still the circulation director. I always loved looking at all of the caricatures on Sardi's walls, everybody from Lucille Ball and any actor and famous playwright you could think of, and even a caricature of my Uncle Nat.

That particular evening we didn't have enough money to pay the bill so they made my husband leave his watch until we could come back with the cash. This was before there was such a thing as a credit card. When I told the story to my Uncle Nat, he said, "You should have just told them to call me and you wouldn't have to had to leave your watch." He thought it was hilarious.

In 1986, I read my Uncle Nat's obituary and other stories about him. Turner Catledge—the man whose shoe laces I had tied and untied under our kitchen table—as managing editor of *The New York Times* had previously said of Nat at a huge dinner honoring him, "If everyone in the world who loved Nat Goldstein loved each other, there would be peace in the world." Nat Goldstein had that wonderful of an influence on so many lives.

An Influence that Endures

Uncle Nat's influence rubbed off on me in several other ways too.

When I was publishing *Broward Life Magazine*, I was in a position to get people tickets to the Sunrise Musical Theater and other events. Maybe my joy in giving came from the joy I would see my father feel when Uncle Nat was able to help him get tickets to something at Madison Square Garden and other places. Nat's outward generosity somehow affected me because I grew up getting so much joy out of meeting people, getting to know them, helping them succeed, and turning them into friends. I still feel that way to this day. It's an important trait to cultivate for success, and it's important for what any one person can do to help another person have more joy in their life.

There was no better role model for this than my Uncle Nat. He seemed to know everybody, and could make anything happen. He was universally loved and respected for his gift of gab and his personal way of connecting with anyone he met. My birth and the birth of my daughter Debbie, and engagement and wedding announcements all found their way into the pages of *The New York Times*.

Uncle Nat seemed bigger than life and his smile could light up a room. I wholeheartedly agree with what Turner Catledge said about peace in the world in his remarks about Nat. He was so dedicated to his job that in the 114-day newspaper strike in the early 1960s, Uncle Nat suffered two heart attacks. He was trying to help get the various lithographer unions and other New York daily newspapers to the bargaining table. He was in it to win it, and I admired him so much. All of us could add a little of his style to our own lives and watch the joy that happens.

When I was on the promotional side of the magazine, it was absolutely a joy to help make people happy. I remember getting our national ad rep tickets to see the Miami Dolphins play the Chicago Bears. He came down from Chicago and I got tickets on the 50-yard line and you would think the man had entered nirvana. It's in the giving not in the receiving that you get the greatest joy, and that has certainly been true for me. (Giving 50-yard line tickets was very Uncle Nat!)

Anticipating Another's Shoe Fit and the Impact

Broward Life won six journalism and graphics awards from the Florida Magazine Association, more than any other magazine our size in the state. In looking at some of our old magazines, I can see part of why we were getting more and more popular. We did include a great many local people in every edition and we got wonderful responses in letters to the editor. We very often took difficult positions on subjects, which created even more interest.

As time went on, we had two of the top advertising sales people from the magazine that didn't want to hire me, come work for us, and we had some great editorial help from freelance editors who had worked for the *Miami Herald*. They were award-winning writers and incredible cartoonists, and as a result our magazine developed a terrific personality.

I always felt like the original people who wouldn't hire me were competitors of mine, even though they really weren't. At one point they got upset that we were growing so rapidly in their territory that they threatened to sue me if I wouldn't disclose proof of my circulation figures, which were being audited by a well known circulation auditing firm out of New York. I remember trying to head that off before it became a big unnecessary issue.

I tried to put myself in my competitors' shoes in terms of what I could do that would have the most impact on them. I had this idea, which I followed through on, to see the attorneys who represented the *Miami Herald* newspaper. I wangled an appointment with one of the partners by saying, "I'll only need 20 minutes of your time."

I told him, "I would like to pay you to write one letter." At first he just laughed at me. "I just need you to write a letter to my competition and just tell them if they'll show us their circulation figures, we'll be glad to show them ours." That's what happened. He wrote a two-line letter, but when they saw it on that particular law firm's letterhead, it ended the whole conversation because that firm had the most powerful publishing attorneys in South Florida and commanded respect.

ᑐOIE-ISM #24

It is a part of growing to experience new ways of being and thinking.
If you liken yourself to some of the world's greatest minds,
you will see similarities. Einstein thought that there was
nothing special about him, except that he was very curious.
Curiosity and creativity are two sides of the same coin.
Don't be afraid to flip it.

ᑐOIE-ISM #25

Turn unstructured time into a most wonderful thing.
I have made wonderful friends taking walks and meeting
people's dogs. The more you can come in contact with other
people and their experiences, the more it broadens your life.
You have no less a brain than Einstein. The question is how you
allow yourself to use the brain you have. Going to a live basketball
game gives me joy today, but when I was younger, I would have
said no thanks. Find a sport or hobby that appeals to you.
Dance like nobody is watching: that's not original from me,
but I love that saying! I'd say that's a great way to live your life.

Joie-ism #26

Make it a practice to remember people's names.
Remember the names of secretaries and executive assistants.
Say their name back to them on the phone. They will then
think they already know you and they should feel some ownership
in the conversation. Remember the names of waitpeople
in restaurants and service industries. Call anyone
with a name badge by that name. Everyone appreciates
being called by their name. Also remember birthdays
whenever you can, people seem to appreciate that.

Joie-ism #27

Assume nothing!
Get the facts before you move forward.

CHAPTER SEVEN

Create Win–Win Situations

JOIE-ISM #28

You must sometimes get beyond your comfort zone
because both sides need to bend a little for find a solution that works.
Everyone gives a little so everyone can gain a lot.

Are You a "Front Person" or a "Back Person"?

A good thing to know about yourself is whether you are a "front person" or a "back person." The distinction is very key for determining where you will feel the happiest and be the most successful in your line of work.

Basically, the front person gets the business in the door, and the back person gets it out. I was a front person in both of my businesses that I describe in this book. The front person meets the public, does public relations, sales, goes to networking events and meetings, gets the reputation of the firm out there, and projects the attributes of the company. The back person works amongst designers, programmers, writers, cooks, number crunchers, and wizards that know what the business is all about. They are the necessary skilled people who are the backbone and structure of the business. Without the back people there is no business. Without the front people there are no sales. Both need to recognize the essential qualities of the other.

Many people today need to play both roles, and more and more people work from home. If the business does not flow in from online sources, somebody has to go out there and get it. An example of a great blend of the front person and back person was when graphic designers worked manually (before computers) at JMG Publishing. We had a job for a real estate developer who wanted to feature his kitchens as the selling point of his homes. Our designer, Kevin, did an outstanding job on the look and flow of the brochure, but something was missing—no pictures or plans of the kitchen.

The best way to get what the client wanted was to compliment Kevin and let him know that the developer loved his design for the brochure, but unfortunately the key selling point was the kitchen; so could he please think about how to include good graphics to highlight the kitchens as the selling point? Yes, he could accept that the client needed the kitchen part included, so he did it.

Had I just looked over his shoulder and said, "Where's the kitchen stuff?" he would have balked, felt that his art was being challenged, and would have reluctantly—but who knows how well—added a bit about the kitchens. By being a front person, I was the liaison to the client and to Kevin, who really was a fine artist working as a graphic designer. The client did not see the design for the brochure until after I had interceded, as I knew without the kitchen it would have been back to the drawing board for us.

Knowing how to best communicate with the person doing the work, what language to use and approach to take, makes the job easier for all concerned, and is another key function of the front person role. If you recognize where you are most comfortable, it is more self-knowledge for you to position yourself in the right job to accomplish your highest good and that can create win-win situations.

What if you are a skilled back person who needs more sales? My first thought is to ask your best clients if there is any more work that you could do for them. If you design, do they need copywriting? You could hire a good copywriter and do more for them. Or, perhaps, there are people doing sales for other firms, not quite like yours, but they can keep you in mind too for the type of work that you are seeking.

If you don't know someone who could be a potential front person for you, do a little front person stuff yourself, no matter how reluctant you are initially, and get out and meet some people who need what you have to offer and be sure to get them to understand that you want more work. Often, the best way is to connect with a company that needs lots of what you do is to become a vendor for them.

You may need to meet with their purchasing agent or department. Ask who to see who can buy your product, and consciously select firms you think you would like to work with. When pitching them, point out that you only have room for one (or a few) more clients, and you have chosen to contact them as you believe that you two are a perfect fit for each other. You don't want everyone as a client (unless you do) but having them feel that they are selected and special could help their decision on doing business with you.

You deliver, you are great at what you do, but you don't always have time to sell more work, as you are busy doing what you do. If you are a skilled front person, go to companies that place their work with a variety of back people.

For us, as previously mentioned, it was the public relations firms and the advertising agencies that turned out to be our biggest sources of business. Another great source of business was people that I met by being involved in civic activities. I would have done the civic activities anyway, as I cared about helping them. Your dedication and enthusiasm will shine through wherever you choose to participate, and there is no need to do something unless you really want to.

It's a win-win if you can get great people more work, and you are compensated for bringing them together. People need all sorts of services that they don't easily find, so you can be the front person in the middle.

Cultivating Trust is a Win-Win

When I first started my magazine, I spent a day with an investor friend going around to different printers in the Miami area. When I walked into Central Litho in Hialeah, Florida, it didn't matter to me what kind of equipment they had because I could intuitively feel they could print my magazine.

I didn't know printing equipment from anything, but their floor was so clean that I thought my God, if you can eat off the floor then they're probably going to be very careful with their printing presses and my publication, which turned out to be exactly true. The man who owned it, Dick, and I developed a trusting relationship.

Initially, Dick would send a bill and we would pay it right away, no problem. But when the summer months came, it was much harder to pay in a timely way, so I had a conversation with him. "How about if I send you part of this now, and we work out a payment thing." That became a win-win for both of us.

Dick would say to me, "It's okay, I trust you. I know how slow it gets in the summer. Just pay as you can."

That was a fortunate break for me and Dick was a special man. He used to have a saying, "AM I right, or am I right?" Sadly, at the age of 48, he died of a massive heart attack after dinner one night. Other people took over and ran it and we never printed the magazine with anyone else but Central Litho.

It's important in your business dealings to work as best as you can with people you have learned to trust. That trust will inevitably be tested, so make sure you always hold up your end of any agreement, whether in writing or in a handshake. Unbreakable trust is a win-win for the success of any business, just as it is with any friendship.

Navigating the Sale of Broward Life Magazine

A tenant who moved into the building where my magazine, *Broward Life*, had its office, was an oil and gas exploration company. The head of it had an office opposite the wall in my office. I could hear him on the phone say, "Well that's the way I do *bidness*. I name my price, you don't like my price, we don't do *bidness*." I'd hear him say those words many times.

As time went on, he developed a real interest in our magazine because he wanted to have articles about his friends placed in it. He would ask us to write flattering stories about people he knew, like local politicians. That wouldn't fly with someone like Bill, our editor. If you wanted a story, you had to be willing to take the truth as he uncovered it, because he was a true journalist and an investigative reporter at heart.

On several occasions we did write things that the oil and gas CEO was interested in, but I doubt he was ever thrilled with everything we wrote. One day he came into my office, sat on my couch, and told me that he was interested in someday maybe owning my magazine. I was really kind of shocked and remembering what I had heard from him behind the wall, I said, "I will tell you this, I'll name my price and if you don't like my price, we won't do business."

He seemed kind of surprised and impressed, and replied, "That's the way I do *bidness* too!"

That's where we left it. Months went by and he came back again to say he was still interested. So, I shot out a number, which to me sounded like an absolutely absurd amount. I had no investment of my own money in this venture, so whatever I said was to me beyond anything anybody would ever pay for it.

I think the figure I gave him was $500,000 or something like that. This was late 1970s dollars. He was a little stunned at the price too, but not long afterward his company became part of a public underwriting of funds for oil and gas exploration. This turned out to be one of the last underwritings their company and this big Wall Street firm had ever done. As a result, he wound up agreeing to my terms and added the magazine on, almost like the tail that wagged the dog, to the oil and gas $10 million underwriting.

I was absolutely thrilled with the sale because I knew I couldn't keep doing it forever and it felt like an ideal time for me to sell while the magazine was still doing well and was still fun to operate. The deal was consummated in November of 1979, and he became the new owner of *Broward Life Magazine*. We did a handshake for me to stay on for a while and run it because he knew nothing about publishing a magazine. I didn't specify a period of time and as the months went by, and we're still making a profit, he had the idea that he probably didn't really need me. He still didn't really understand what a publisher did, so he made Bill both the editor and publisher and eliminated my position.

It has always been my strong belief that you don't have the keyboard and the checkbook in the same publishing office. The person in charge of getting to a bottom line of profit is different, with different priorities, from the person who is interested in getting to the bottom line of a story. The short of it is the new owner's arrangement didn't work. I got a call from him and he asked, "How come when you were in charge it was making money, and now it isn't?"

"Ralph, maybe now you know what a publisher does."

Not long after that, my old competitor, *Gold Coast* magazine, bought the publication from him. Come full circle, they wouldn't hire me years earlier, but they ultimately, though indirectly, bought me out!

Giving Something Extra to Create a Win-Win

We kept rocking and rolling and the work kept coming in for JMG Publishing. We cultivated repeat work as we catered to public relations and advertising agency firms entrusted with doing the collateral materials for their clients. The collateral is what our graphic artists designed, and then we printed it.

The profit was in the printing and the reorders of the same brochure or letterhead. That gave us leverage to make the graphic design much more competitive with those firms that did not do the printing or the entire package. This is key to positioning your company, or your product: do more than one essential component of what your client needs.

It makes the most sense to specialize when you can count on volume. That is why the reorders from the printing jobs were pretty much all profit. We made our investment back on the initial printing and design package, but then, all the reorders were gravy. What I could not print in house, due to it being multi-colored or larger than our presses could handle, I simply jobbed out and bought the press downtime from a printer who had the perfect equipment for my job. We supplied the paper and film for them to make their own printing plates. This was a win-win situation as they sold their press downtime and both of us benefited from the reorders.

Sometimes you have to look at an opportunity from a different perspective to see the win-win angle. Key to this, in the history of JMG Publishing, was our incredible experience with Motorola.

Motorola was uniquely positioned in South Florida as a dream client for printing companies, in that it only approved three printing vendors to do ALL of their local work. I had taken the entire purchasing department of Motorola to lunch at the fanciest restaurant in Fort Lauderdale, and all those guys were thrilled to eat there. There must have been nine of us sitting at a round table, and I told them how much I wanted them as a client, and we would be glad to prioritize their work if they ever needed something fast.

What I told them turned out to be prophetic, as one Monday before the traditional Thanksgiving break, I got a call from one of my purchasing department buddies at Motorola. He said he had an urgent job due to a product recall, and he had to have delivery the Monday after Thanksgiving. Would we be open over the holiday to do their work?

We had planned to be closed for Thanksgiving just like everybody else. But we were not like everybody else when I told him, "Let me ask my guys if they would be willing to work over the holiday."

Each of Motorola's other printing vendors, both large ones in Miami, had already told them that they would be closed. This presented me with an opportunity. I queried my guys by saying, "Would you like to make your entire Christmas money by working over Thanksgiving?"

I promised to pay my employees triple holiday time and make the job over Thanksgiving a fun happening with food and music, as we worked practically around the clock. The consensus was that if they could make enough extra money to make it worthwhile, they were willing to give it a shot.

I called Motorola back and told them we have three pricing levels and schedules: regular; rush, which is double; and MIRACLE, where you are not allowed to even ask a price. This job qualifies as a MIRACLE. I told them I had no idea what it would cost, but the guys were willing to do it if they made out exceptionally well with their paychecks.

We started on the design work for a one-page, two-color flyer, as we had several two color presses, and wanted to create something that would be easy to print. We also had to consider what paper stock we could get fast to compliment what we already had in-house. The quantity they needed exceeded what we could possibly deliver in a few days, but they agreed to the suggestion that we keep feeding them, starting Monday morning, until all of the zillion flyers were delivered.

Since we were the only company even willing to work for them over the holiday, they acquiesced to our demands. We got to work and did what we could to have our guys comfortable doing the long shifts. We somehow secured enough boxes to initially get them enough flyers to load a truck that made multiple trips on that Monday, Tuesday and Wednesday, following Thanksgiving.

Motorola was thrilled. They had their recall information about the product out into the world, and we were delighted to come through for them. The guys made out well so it was definitely a big win-win situation for everyone. How easy it would have been to just say that we would be closed from the Wednesday before Thanksgiving through the holiday weekend. That's what all the other vendors did, but we had learned how to create win-win deals that elevated us above the competition.

My point here is that opportunity can present itself when you least expect it, and you must be willing to do things a little outside the box. No way was our equipment the most economical for them for this job, but hey, we were the only ones willing to run with it.

An added perk for everyone was that Motorola was so delighted with our caring response to their immediate need, they continued to give us as much work as we could handle. They loved us and we loved them. We printed an annual magazine type book for them, and they didn't even seek another bid. We were also keeping a lot of other printers happy with all the work we farmed out from Motorola.

Regular, Rush and *Miracle* became our playful lingo reference points for quoting jobs, and everyone in our company and Motorola was delighted with our relationship. How did it happen? We were just willing to do something different from any of their other vendors.

A tradition I carried on with all of my businesses was elf week. My assistant Brenda and I would make these elaborate sleds full of goodies, drinks and things, and deliver them to our clients. These were huge, well decorated gorgeous sleighs and big gifts. We did that every year. Believe you me, our clients remembered and appreciated those gifts, and it was always a win-win for us when they reciprocated in some way.

Once I sold my businesses, it felt funny not having something to do like that around the holidays. So, to this day, I have always kept the tradition of elf week alive in the second week of December. I love giving gifts to people, many of whom have no idea or expectation of getting any.

It is one way of showing the seasonal spirit and I love giving people joy. Every elf week, for all these decades, I still wear the same red Victoria's Secret jacket as I did in the 70's and 80's.

Bringing Reluctant Partners Together

Crime Stoppers is a national organization that was founded in Albuquerque, New Mexico because of a need for local witnesses, or people with information or leads about crimes to be able to come forward anonymously, as most people were reluctant to contact law enforcement simply because they did not want to get involved. The anonymous tip line was born. Due to the fear and apathy on the part of most of the public, the pot was sweetened by offering cash awards that could be as much as $1,000 for a tip leading to conviction. The idea took hold, and it soon began to spread across the country. When I first heard of this organization, it was because they were making inroads in Texas.

One of my key civic-minded businessman buddies asked me to help bring Crime Stoppers to Florida and specifically, to Broward County. We approached the local sheriff's office, and they were understandably not too comfortable with getting the public involved in police work. Eventually, we went to Washington D.C., as our sheriff had become a congressman, and the three of us had dinner and reached an agreement to bring the program to our local county. It was important for us to have the former sheriff's blessing, which we used as leverage with the new sheriff who then became more receptive to the idea.

I served on the first Crime Stoppers board and was initially very enthusiastic. I would attend the meetings with police officers and an occasional detective. They would list the disposition of cases, and also describe new cases they wanted to let the public know about. Our tip line was soon buzzing! The program had some initial success, soon stabilized, but it wasn't building any great momentum at that time. I heard firsthand from police officers that they were disgruntled that crime reporters would jump the gun and report things in the newspaper that they weren't ready for the public to know.

I heard this grumbling for months and decided to do something about it. I may have done this event under the auspices of Crime Stoppers, or the umbrella of the Broward Workshop, as this was in the early 1980s, and I was just in the early stages of building JMG Publishing. I knew almost all of the members of the local media, and many Florida politicians.

Those who had ever, or would likely be the ones to report on local crime, were invited to a sort of meet and greet with the local police officers and sheriff's deputies. This took some doing—like trying to fit ten pounds of feathers in a five-pound bag! I pulled out all the stops on my persuasion abilities and gathered them in a nice room that had refreshments.

Law enforcement supported my efforts because of my enthusiasm and work with the Crime Stoppers program. The reporters knew Bill, our editor at the magazine, and many of them knew me as well. Most all of the other media people knew us both. Picture a sixth-grade dance with the girls on one side of the room and the boys on the other. Each group stayed closely knit, looked at their watches a lot and counted the minutes for the event to be over. Fearless me welcomed them all, and asked them to line up on each side of the room. Then I said, "Okay, all the media people please take two steps forward." Then I got the cops and deputies to follow suit.

It was funny to see, but it was no laughing matter that they were so reluctant to meet one another. My big pitch was that if they knew the face behind their respective roles, and personally knew each other by name, they could contact each other with information and develop a rapport as to what would be okay to release to the public, and what confidential information would be provided first to a trusted source. We were locked in that room for about three hours as I went around and dragged some of them to meet the other side. I did my best to convince them that mutual trust would develop if they made the effort to know one another.

Some law enforcement personnel cited specific cases that were hindered by the early release of information. I also got a reporter to explain to the other side about the reality of deadlines and why they had to write in a timely manner to make the next day's paper. A local television anchor detailed the parameters of the lead time needed before a story could be broadcast in that medium. By the end of their time together they were tentatively shaking hands and taking each other's business cards, as I moved around like Tinkerbell trying to get them to loosen up and join the program. I stressed their mutual interest in getting the facts right and in a timely way.

Ultimately, it did make a good difference and there were some cops and reporters that I knew who did develop a relationship that was mutually beneficial. I helped to create a win-win, not only for the police and the media, but also for Crime Stoppers and the entire citizenry of Broward County.

Use the Joy of Giving to Create Win-Win

It was always important to me to give the same courtesy to the lowest paid employee as the highest. People in the printing industry, who typically were not among the highest paid were those who worked in the bindery. Ironically, if they screwed up then the whole job had to been done over. When I was in the printing business, bindery workers made between $4 and $5 an hour.

One such applicant came to me with his long hair carefully hidden in a ponytail, tucked into the collar of his long-sleeved white shirt, which covered his tattooed arms. He was polite and very much needed a job, so we hired him for the bindery and soon he was a valuable employee who cared about doing the job right. Once when he was working the night shift, he left a note, "I 'mest' up" as he did not complete a particular job correctly.

I hung around to speak with him when he came in the next night. "You know, John, you are a great guy in the bindery, but you are young, and if you ever want to get better jobs you have to learn some basic stuff, like spelling."

He slouched and lowered his head, and I could tell that he felt embarrassed. I continued to compliment his work ethic and asked him if he would like to continue his education. He quickly said, "No, I don't like school."

It turned out he had never finished high school. He kept working for us, but the English teacher in me could not help but want to see him learn more so that one day he would have a better shot at a better job, and a better life. A few months went by and I had learned of a remedial class at a local junior college that helped people like John.

"What do you think about taking a college class?" I asked him.

He looked at me like I must be confused, but I told him about this class and offered to pay the tuition for him. At that offer, he seemed genuinely grateful for the opportunity. He went to the class, did well in it, and went on to take other classes.

John became a key and loyal employee and could be counted on to work any hours to get a job out. On one occasion, an annual report had to be delivered on July 5th, which meant someone had to be working in the bindery over the July 4th weekend. No problem for us, as John was happy to do it. My interceding to help this kid improve his education paid off for him and he soon developed a lot more confidence so that he wasn't afraid to leave an occasional note.

He was truly appreciative and to this day I feel really good that I helped him out. It underscored my belief that the real joy is in the giving, and when it is unexpected by someone, it makes the giving that much sweeter.

JOIE-ISM #29

Give them a reason to want to say YES!
When I was pushing to get an appointment with somebody,
I really felt and expressed that I had something of benefit for
them and wanted to give them the opportunity to know about it.
I realized that rejection doesn't mean anything.
If someone says no ten times, it doesn't mean
the eleventh time they won't say yes.

JOIE-ISM #30

You have to show somebody why they need
what you offer and show them what the benefit is.
If you ask anybody whether they want to buy such and such,
the immediate reaction is usually, "No, I don't need it."
So you must be prepared and anticipate every objection with a
detailed response demonstrating how they can benefit from it.

JOIE-ISM #31

If you're going to have your own business,
you should never burn bridges when you quit or change jobs.
This is true for life in general, but particularly true if
you want to be successful in business.

JOIE-ISM #32

Enthusiasm sells!
Selling is nothing more than overcoming objections,
and a great tool for accomplishing that is enthusiasm.
It was always my secret weapon. People love being around
positive energy, which helps to break down resistance.

CHAPTER EIGHT

Pick Smart People and Let Them Do Their Jobs

JOIE-ISM #33

*Hire the best and the brightest and then trust them to do their job.
Otherwise, that lack of trust will result in micro-managing
which will drain the life out of your business and out of you.*

Everyone's Growth Grows the Company

When I was publishing *Broward Life Magazine*, I would often be asked, "And what do youuuuu write?" Invariably their lips were pursed, or the eyebrows askew. I would politely shrug, "Mostly checks!"

That was the actual truth. I was so busy selling advertising and making sure that the payroll would be met that I often neglected to even read the magazine.

The first time I met my husband Lew was at an advertising agency Christmas cocktail party. I said, "Your name sounds familiar."

"Yes, I was in your magazine."

"Oh," I said, "I never read it."

From that unlikely exchange, a lifelong love bloomed. I actually can't say I "never" read it, but when I was looking through old copies to jog my memory for this book, I was constantly remarking, "WOW! This is great writing! I love this magazine!"

A lot of credit for the magazine's quality has to go to Bill Luening, the editor. He really upgraded the publication from fluff to substance. I recall a newspaper article about me that said I brought the magazine from puffery to substance, but it was actually "Willie Willie" (my personal affectionate nickname for Bill) who created this change. He was a true journalist, and no ticket to anything in town or any other freebie would ever tempt him to betray his journalistic standards.

"No," he would say, when offered free tickets to something. "I need to write without being influenced by gifts or perks of any kind."

As for me, I was happy to distribute tickets for headliners appearing at the Sunrise Theatre, which attracted the same entertainers often seen on TV and in Las Vegas.

When I sold a twelve-page full color advertising contract to a local restaurant, Bill, agreeing with our restaurant editor, unfortunately did not give them a great review. To him, the public had a right to know what kind of food was being served, and how the quality compared to other restaurants. But my attitude about this friction between advertising and journalistic truth was to explain it away with a bit of humor: "I'm surrounded by assassins."

"Couldn't you just wait and review them in a few months?" an exasperated me would plead when these conflicts occurred. "Their ad was scheduled for this month." But Bill was unwavering in his high standards and I respected that. He practiced true journalism and believed in the public's right to know.

While I got the credit for upgrading the magazine, it was Bill's work that won us all the journalism awards. This is a fine example of what I mean when I say hire people smarter than you, better at doing what they do than anyone else you could hire, and let them do their work unhindered. Of course you get the credit when the effort is successful, but you also get the blame when something doesn't come out as planned.

That is a worthwhile risk to take, as no organization grows when the boss tries to control everything. A team is required for most businesses to be successful—you are the boss and the team's cheerleader, but not the one to fill every role required to make your organization a continued success.

If you have employees, let them be a part of decision-making whenever possible. People need a sense of ownership in the process and it definitely benefits everybody when people who work for you feel like they are working WITH you.

Whenever you can, be mindful of delegating tasks, work, decisions and anything that enables others to feel their own power within your company or work situation. You cannot grow if you hold tight and try to control everything, because nobody else will feel like they are a part of the process and your controlling tightness will result in your organization shrinking, not expanding. If it isn't growing or changing, it's stagnant. You may just find that your best ideas are inspired by someone else's.

If you hire someone, or assign a task to someone who knows more about it than you do, you GROW, the company grows and everyone is better off to have tapped into the knowledge that this person has and you don't. Be smart enough to know when someone knows more than you do.

It helps that you like them, but if a particular skill is needed, the skill set is the higher priority over liking them for seeing your best results. If they perform well, guess who gets the credit? YOU! Again, the downside is if they screw up then you get the blame.

Be the Boss without Being Bossy

It's always important to talk across, not down, to employees and clients.

Not everyone gets to be the head of a company, but many people are the heads of departments, sections, divisions and so forth. Even in our places of worship, boards and hierarchies often appoint a person to be the one having the power to affect and change things. If this is you, here are some thoughts I would like to share.

An effective boss is one who listens. Really listens. If there is a problem or a situation where you find that competent and reliable people are voluntarily leaving without a seemingly real reason, perhaps it is time to look in the mirror.

Are you always in the mix when things are not going right? Do you tend to blame other people for things that you really need to fix? Do you try to control every aspect of the work that flows through your department? Do you hire people you think make you look good, but may not be the brightest or most talented for the job?

It is critical to success that you surround yourself with the "best and brightest" and once you do, they will make you shine. If you dumb down your group, guess what? Your smarter and more talented people will get bored, frustrated, and eventually seek a new job, a new church, a new community or a new whatever it is. No one likes to feel like their contributions are sidestepped and ignored.

It's absolutely essential that you leave the lines of communication open and allow those who are a part of your organization to contribute their thoughts and ideas for the greater good. A compliment or an acknowledgment from you will mean more than you think. And most important to me, and hopefully you will concur, is that you don't forget what you agreed to. If you don't keep your word, or forget you even gave your word about an event or circumstance, be prepared to be resented, shunned and shuttled off to a faraway place in the minds of your associates.

Nothing says you don't care more than forgetting what you told someone you would do. It was a clever concept for a book, *All I Really Need to Know I Learned in Kindergarten* by Robert Fulghum, but it really has meaning here. Treat people well, engage in meaningful conversation with an eye to understanding how you are being perceived, and you will connect better with your co-workers, congregants, students or whomever, and will reap the benefits of being surrounded by people with a vested interest in what happens in your organization. Once a person feels they are not valued, not heard, or hear only lip service and absent-minded agreement from you, you are in trouble, whether you realize it or not.

"Nothing succeeds like success," goes the old saying, and you get that by cheerleading your team in a way that each person knows they have value and something to contribute to your goals and ambitions and to advance the entire group or organization.

Making the Case You're the Right Person for the Job

When you are the smart person needing to be picked for the right job, you obviously must make the right and best case for yourself. There is an old saying, "You can't redo a first impression." Be sure that your job interview is with the best person who can understand how you can be a benefit to their company and its vision.

Experience and training is vital for many jobs, and there are also opportunities to be hired if you are qualified to be doing that particular job for the first time. But it means you have to give the impression that you are a skilled quick learner and super-interested in this one specific job that is being offered. If specific skills are required, be sure your interviewers are convinced that you have them, or can learn them.

You need to sell the interviewer on taking a chance with you and you need to make the interviewer feel positive about you joining their firm. Throughout my career I looked at hundreds of artist portfolios and was primarily concerned with the variety of someone's graphic design abilities, as this is where I felt I was making the biggest contribution. You as the prospect need to present your work and yourself with care. It goes without saying you need to look clean and neat, but I realize that dress codes have shifted drastically over the past few decades. Guys we hired for the pressroom did not have to appear as fashionably put together as someone applying for a customer service or desk job, especially if they would be meeting clients. Everyone needs to be presentable.

My biggest tip in getting the job you want is do your homework and find out as much as you can about the products, values and needs of the company where you are seeking employment. If you are familiar with their clients, that can be very helpful. Act like you could fit right in. Instead of dwelling too long about what they want, presume that they need you and your skill set or you would not have applied to them. Be assertive as to why you want that particular job, and tell them stuff that shows you have looked into their website, or customer base, or product, or whatever makes you personally familiar with their needs.

If you seem ready to take any job that is available, you are giving off subliminal vibes that won't seem as strong to this particular interviewer, because being willing to take any job distances you from the sincerity of wanting that one job. They are looking for someone who is the best candidate for the job that the interview is about. Possibly you could accept a lesser job in a given department with the idea of moving up when they have an opening, but otherwise stick to your goals for the specific kind of job you want.

Wow them with your knowledge of why you are a uniquely perfect fit for their job. This entails knowing what they need. Selling the benefits of yourself as an employee is always meaningful. Can you work late? How much flexibility is there in your hours or days or weekends to meet their needs? If you know someone they like and do business with, it's worth mentioning that person during the interview. As many ways as you can find to connect to the person interviewing you, the better.

If you know something in particular about what they choose to hang on their walls, or perhaps something visible on their desk, discussing it may be a small, but useful way of connecting with them. The more they can be comfortable seeing you fitting into their organization, the better for you. If they have a family photo with a son or daughter and you have a child of a similar age, mention that and make small talk around it. Make it professional, but a little personal touch sets you apart from the other applicants.

The key is to stay focused and answer questions succinctly and truthfully. Not a good idea to ramble on. Speak in a distinct clear way, be careful not to mumble and say "uh" too many times. This person will likely decide if you are a prospect for them within the first minute or two of chatting with you. Are you presenting yourself as being confident that you can do this job? Are you saying anything that lets them know you are reliable? This needs to be a big YES. Eagerness to start, or to be able to start as soon as they need you is ideal.

If you are leaving another job and have to give notice, never offer to shorten the notice. KEEP YOUR WORD to your existing or former employer, and that will give your prospective employer a good feeling about your ability to do as you say. *Keeping your word is key in any situation.* Every employer wants someone who is trustworthy.

Hone in on your particular skills that sets you apart. Sometimes it can be a big plus to have letters of reference from people your interviewer respects. If you happen to have worked for a competitor of the company you are now applying to, it is important to carefully consider your interviewer's feelings about that. Perhaps they will think you are loyal to old friends at your old company. It is important to state your reasons for preferring to work for the new company, especially if both companies share the same market. Use your intuition and trust your feelings about what it is you think makes the most sense to emphasize. Whatever the position, tailor your comments to the widest range of skills you are able to offer.

For example, if you do graphics, discuss the range of logos you can do, your skill with color, the computer programs you are proficient in, and anything else that shows you are the best fit for them. If it is a job that involves very specific software to have expertise in, be sure to let them understand the degree to which you have mastered that particular software. The more you can make yourself indispensable the better. For me and the artists I interviewed, a great plus was their range of creativity.

Go in there and project a positive image that you are an asset, and present an attitude of you *CAN* and *WILL* do this job. Many job interviews today have the initial contact online. If this is the case for the job you want, you will need to have your resume or written materials speak for you. My tip here is that the document you send has really good spacing so that they can easily read blocks of information about you. If there is too much verbiage compacted together, it is less likely it will be read. People who have to look through a whole lot of resumes will be attracted to ones in which they can easily see your name and qualifications for the particular job you are seeking. You may need to tailor what you send to each company. Rarely will the same resume work for all the jobs you apply for, so make them as personal and personable as you can. Your contact information has to be easily seen.

There are many resources on the internet that can show you how to best prepare a resume style which is effective to catch the attention of a prospective employer. If your interview is initially done electronically, make sure they can easily sense your joy and desire to work for them. This also needs to come through in what you write in making the case for why you want the job. We are all individuals and no two people will do things exactly the same way, so be sure you let them know you can do the job, you want to do the job, and you can do it well!

Hands Across Broward Was Amazing and Unprecedented

Here is an example of an event where I needed to pick the smartest people and simply facilitate letting them do their jobs. When I found myself elected president of the United Way in our county, it seemed that I needed to do more, be more, and make the upcoming year special. Prior presidents had been men and all had done a good job, but none did more than expected. I thought that being a woman, I needed to make my term of office more special and memorable.

In that spirit I contacted my good friend Gary Bitner of the then public relations firm Bitner, Laurenti & Pierson. Both Gary and Lynn Laurenti were special friends and we did lots of favors for one another. Today Gary heads the Bitner Group with offices in Fort Lauderdale and Orlando, Florida. Gary and I went to lunch at the Bonaventure Country Club, and while munching salads we came up with the idea that we needed to do a special event to bring awareness to the United Way of Broward County. From that innocent lunch we contacted all of the main advertising agencies and public relations firms in Broward and invited them to attend a meeting. I told the executives from these companies that we needed just an hour of their time and promised not to bother them again, unless they were so turned on by what happened at the meeting and wanted to participate more.

We all met in the conference room of the United Way in early 1985, and the idea was to toss out ideas for a countywide event that would highlight the United Way and the good work that it did in our community. Wild ideas were thrown out, along with some cautions and exclamations of "How the hell can we do that?" I am not sure who suggested it first, perhaps it was Gary, but someone mentioned holding an event at the beach. The idea grew from there to getting thousands of people to line the Broward County beaches and hold hands. I added, and "we can all hold a red ribbon," as I was always conscious of the photo ops and thought a prop like a red ribbon would make it truly memorable and awesome. My very superstitious grandma Rose always would put a red ribbon on a crib or carriage believing it would bring good luck. We would need all the luck we could get. I had a red ribbon ingrained in me as a wonderful symbol. At the close of the meeting that became our plan.

Someone figured out that in order to not have a break in the line we would need 40,000 people to participate. My job was to make this happen. At dinner with friends, my husband Lew tossed around the question of where do you get a ribbon that many miles long? We learned from our dinner companion, who was a retired army reserve general, about a ribbon company in New England that had done extensive buntings and ribbons for the military. When I called, I said to the receptionist that I had a really weird request for a ribbon. She transferred me to someone who made my day when he got on the line: "This is Joe in the Weird Department."

After much discussion with Joe, it was decided to order 23 miles of ribbon that was 5 inches wide, rolled so it could fit on a roll to be transported to Florida. I thought it could be one ribbon, but there is no way a truck was able to hold such a thing. When the ribbon arrived in South Florida via UPS, we did a photo op opening the back of the truck to reveal numerous huge rolls of ribbon being rolled out of the truck. They were delivered to a warehouse owned by Florida Power & Light where we could distribute and staple it all together the night before the event. When we rolled out all of these gigantic rolls of red ribbon off the back of the UPS truck, that became a media event itself because that was pretty unusual. The media probably wouldn't have reported it if they didn't have the photo to go with the event preparation.

Disregarding the Naysayers

Whoever said it couldn't be done, we had just shrugged and continued to work on this wild idea. It had taken nine months, and I had donated the full-time talents of one of my graphic designers, Leah, who did a terrific job designing the logo of Hands Across Broward, designing the ads we ran in local papers to encourage people to attend, and designing posters and whatever else was needed. Rick Ott, who was a key marketing guy from the *Fort Lauderdale News*, did an awesome job getting the event well covered in the newspaper. Gary Bitner and his firm also worked tirelessly to help bring this wild idea to fruition and his company won an award for their efforts.

Since Broward County was comprised of many cities and municipalities, we had our work cut out for us in coordinating everyone. Rick was essential to getting all of these diverse communities on board. It did take us nine months from the day of the first meeting brainstorming ideas until the actual event happened. Diverse communities worked together to sign up participants and the idea caught on and created a feeling of fun and unity for the county to have a wonderful experience and promote the United Way. I learned that if there is a hesitancy on the part of one prospective participant, the knowledge that so many others were already on board was the best way to get 100 percent participation, and we succeeded in doing that.

Early in the planning for Hands Across Broward the committee thought it would be great to have some kind of action signal to all participants that the ribbon was up. Our executive director of United Way, Doug, asked the office of Governor Bob Graham if the governor would like to ride in a helicopter across the 23 miles of beach to signal that the event was a success. The response we received was that he had a scheduling conflict.

We then asked Broward County Sheriff Nick Navarro if he would be interested. Nick jumped at the chance and loved the idea. A few days before the event was to take place, Doug received a call from the governor's office saying that he would be able to fly in the helicopter at the event after all. Doug called me all excited to announce that yes, the governor could be there. I reminded Doug that the governor had originally said no, and there was no way that it would be fair to replace the sheriff, who had been our supporter for months.

"Are you telling me that you are turning down the governor of the state of Florida?" howled Doug through the phone.

"He was the one who turned us down. I don't see any way that we can be in integrity and disappoint the sheriff with a change of plans at the last minute."

The ribbon was placed along the beach and at precisely 11 a.m. on the day of the event, everyone grabbed the ribbon in front of them and raised it up at the same time. In addition to Broward's 23 miles of beach, there were inlets where boats or divers were positioned, and the many photos of the divers holding the ribbon across the Hillsboro Inlet were amazing!

It was Sheriff Navarro who was cheering and waving as the ribbon was raised across the coastline. It is more important to keep our word. There was no win-win to renegotiate this and I believe we did the right thing.

Here is how the *Miami Herald* reported the story on October 6, 1985:

> From the towering apartments shadowing
> Hallandale Beach to the Barefoot Mailman Lounge
> on Hillsboro Mile, some 60,000 Broward residents
> joined hands, glanced skyward as the sirens
> screamed and, at the 11 o'clock chime, raised high
> the red ribbon that spanned 23 miles of coast in a
> dramatic show of support for the United Way.

I was quoted in the article as saying, "Who said we couldn't do it in Broward? It's a wonderful spirited event. It's been terrific."

Our event was unprecedented, and yes, it spawned even bigger ideas! The next year, in May 1986, a *Hands Across America* event occurred during which an estimated 6.5 million people held hands in a human chain across the U.S., raising about $34 million for local charities to combat hunger and homelessness. The chain linked major cities, and in places the chain was six to ten people deep. The people from Hands Across America did come to talk to us, so we know our event was the impetus for theirs. A lot of good came from these events so all the effort was worthwhile.

One thing I learned from our event is if there is no photo opportunity, a lot doesn't get reported. If you really want to make a difference for a cause, you need to put thought into creating a photo op, making signs, going out there and saying what you want to say. But also engage your local media (including social media) to cover your event because that's how news is created today. It often has to have a strong visual component in order to interest them.

ℐOIE-ISM #34

Always take pride in what you do.
Before GPS, London taxi drivers had to pass a test on knowing
all of the city streets and the shortest routes between them.
They were being the best they could be. Taking pride in what you
do, whether you think it's a menial task or not, will enrich your life.

Joie-ism #35

*If you have employees, let them be a part
of decision-making whenever possible.*
People need a sense of "ownership" in the process
and it definitely benefits everybody when people who
work for you feel like they are working WITH you.
People will do more than they think they can if you
make them feel important and make them feel like
what they are doing really matters.

Joie-ism #36

*Whenever you can, be mindful of delegating
tasks, work, decisions and anything that enables others
to feel their own power within your company or situation.*
You cannot grow if you hold tight and try to control everything.
No one else will feel like they are a part of the process, and your
controlling tightness will result in your organization shrinking,
not expanding. If it isn't growing or changing, it's stagnant.
You may just find that your best ideas are
inspired by someone else's.

Joie-ism #37

*Be smart enough to know when someone
knows more than you do.*
If you hire someone, or assign a task to someone
who knows more about it than you do, you GROW,
the company grows and everyone is better off to have
tapped into the knowledge that this
person has and you don't.

CHAPTER NINE

Taking the Courageous Step

JOIE-ISM #38

Star in your own movie! Are you in charge of your life?
Are you the actor or are you reacting to what happens in your life?
You are the director of your life, you are
the actor, the producer, you are it!

Stay Open to a Sense of Awe

I have always appreciated quality, sophistication and aesthetics. The first thing I always want to do when I arrive in Paris is walk into Notre-Dame Cathedral and just sit there in awe, which is how I feel about all of the big cathedrals of Europe. They show that what man can conceive, man can achieve.

I was in a Costco and a man came behind me and said, "Read that book, it's one of the best." *The Pillars of the Earth* by Ken Follett is about the building of Salisbury Cathedral which began in medieval Britain. It took about 750 years to build! The only reason I bought the book was that I trusted if the Universe comes in with a suggestion and a stranger tells you something like that, the Universe is using that man as a messenger. I ended up loving that book.

Another time I was in a metaphysical bookstore in Southern California looking for a gift for my daughter Debbie, and a book fell off a shelf, literally in front of me. It was about 11:11, written by Solara, and a very way-out book. But I loved it and got interested in all kinds of esoteric spiritual things as a result. It was awe-inspiring that the book literally fell into my lap. There wasn't anything subtle about that occurrence at all.

Sometimes it's vital in life to have those multiple levels of awareness because you never know what's going to fall into your lap. You never know who you're going to meet, who you're going to talk to, or what's going to happen. I have found the neatest people standing in line waiting to get into a restaurant. That happened in Paris with a man who is still my friend on Facebook.

I talk to everybody. That has added so much to my life. You just never know where the next gift is coming from, or the next person who says, "Have you tried this on the menu?" I might normally say, "No, I don't think I would like that," but I have learned to just try it, and if it doesn't appeal to me, I can choose never to eat it again. The important thing is to always keep yourself open to new experiences.

Don't Let Old Age Thinking Hold You Back

If I were to match the trombones in the musical "The Music Man" year for year, then I enjoyed the year that they all would be playing loudly! To celebrate my 76th birthday, I climbed a tree with my granddaughter as part of a hike we both did with my daughter in Lithia Park, in Ashland, Oregon. It's exciting to be at a place in life where you can focus on the fun, and like Pablo Picasso said, "One starts to get young at sixty."

I have always been reluctant to say how old I was, as many of my friends are much younger. The people I hike with are mostly in their 50s, and some don't know my age, as I thought they would think I couldn't keep up, climb, or do the complete hike. That is not the case, although I admit when in the high temperatures, a desire for a shorter, less strenuous hike often seems like a wonderful idea.

It is this perception around age that has prompted me to hold back, or just to avoid the subject of age all together. I remember that many years ago, at some type of promotional cocktail party function, I was enjoying a great conversation with a young man. We were laughing and the spirit of the evening was one of fun, although it was an event to promote the sales of a drink, and this person worked in marketing for the drink company.

When the subject of age inadvertently came up, I undoubtedly said what mine was . . . sixty something . . . and he reacted by saying, "What? Am I talking to my mother here?"

His reaction was a shock and a disappointment, but I was so influenced by this chance encounter that I never again revealed my age to a much younger person. Now I realize that it was his problem all along. What's the difference if you are having a fun conversation? Who cares how old you are!

Age can be a state of mind, yet, we do have to respect that the body does change. My philosophy is to be as youthful in my thinking as I can be, for as long as I can, and so be it.

Never think you are too old for something. That is a totally man-made societal influence and truly means nothing. I remember a man who celebrated his 90th birthday with the dedication of a bench in his honor, at the top of one of the trails we used to climb together in Carmel Valley.

A great secret to aging gracefully is to be grateful for all the joys in your life. Focus on the good things and appreciate your years as a gift. If someone has a hard time with an older friend, well, there are plenty out there who would welcome a chance to enjoy experiences with someone they find fun to be with, no matter what their age.

Besides, in dog years we are all ancient, and who thinks about the age of a dog when it expresses love, both with its eyes and heart, just like many of the older folks you encounter.

Whatever your age is right now, if you feel like you missed out on something, there is no time like the present to act. You're not too old, except in your perceptions of yourself. Once people used to think of 50 as being old, but now 50 is young. Wait till you're 70 and you'll see how young 50 really is.

Let me give you an illustration involving how I released the artist within me. The close proximity of Idyllwild to Palm Springs,

California made it a beautiful ride up to the mountains from the desert floor. Idyllwild has cabins, a few great restaurants and an abundance of fabulous people who host workshops, spiritual gatherings, music events, and art classes. I love going there.

Retired nun, educator and author Francis Rothluebber was one of the facilitators who worked with individuals and groups. Her focus was the study and practice of evolutionary spirituality. She was the co-founder of Spirit Mountain Retreat Center and would host me and others in our group one Saturday every month on a variety of life process topics.

I met all sorts of creative wonderful people by attending her special events, including the mandala artist Paul Heussenstamm (Mandalas.com). Paul became very special to me, and I refer to him as "my soul brother." He paints exquisite mandalas and sacred art, and leads workshops that have taught me and thousands of other people to paint our own mandalas. You could do it too. Paul is doing workshops all over the world, and everyone who attends leaves having done a fabulous mandala. Look him up. His art really is exciting.

I found myself so surprised at the art I was able to create, after participating in just one of the many workshops I attended, that soon I began to offer to paint personal mandalas based on a person's key interest, astrological sign or whatever they wanted the theme to be. I sold many of them when we lived in Carmel Valley and had a beautiful art studio set up in our house. Living near the art mecca of Carmel, I found myself attending wonderful art workshops with local artists and discovered a new confidence in my work. A gallery in Carmel chose my work to be included in a juried exhibition they were doing on abstract art, and that encouraged me to sell my work and create more mandalas. I even have a website on Fine Art America, which is a wonderful way for any level of artist to share their work. (My own website is Joie-Goodkin.artistwebsites.com)

I continue to have fun exploring new mediums and while I was writing this book, took a class in acrylic pouring. That was so wonderful that I bought some supplies and plan on doing it in my home studio, which is along a wall in my garage. Many friends find a corner in their home or garage and let the creativity fly.

There is no need to feel restricted by space or by thinking that your art isn't good enough. Good enough for who? For what? If this is something you have always wanted to do, go for it. Whatever might hold you back from trying new things, consciously reframe in your mind so that you are able to free yourself to try whatever it is that is calling you. I don't think we are ever too old or too busy or too anything to set aside some personal time to pursue things that we keep putting off. Procrastination is often a sign of thinking that you have to do something perfectly to do it at all.

Well, guess what? Perfect, like everything else, is in the eye of the beholder. Get out your paints, wood carving tools, writing journal, clay, or whatever it might be and give yourself permission to experience something new. The joy of being creative is something we can all experience, no matter our age.

It's all about perspective and as you age, just allow yourself to feel like you can grow better, grow wiser. Take care of yourself enough so you retain the ability to do what you want. Look at all of the information available about the value of exercise. Even if you take two fifteen-minute walks a day, you're doing so much to improve your body, mind, and spirit. There is as much information as you need available on the internet to maximize your awareness and your health at any age.

While age may just be a number, I do respect the number. As you get older, when you're 68 or so, you look in the mirror and think who the hell let the air out of my face? None of it really means anything in the bigger scheme of things if you are finding fulfillment in your life.

If it's too painful to look in the mirror, then don't look in the mirror unless you absolutely have to. It's that easy. The only one who is really that concerned about it is you. Other people look at you and probably never realize you were once 25 years old. They probably think you always looked like this. You know better. You know you're a composite of all those factors that made you who you are. If you liken yourself to a recipe, combining all of your rich experiences of life, my God, just imagine you're still a tasty, savory dish.

Everything you need to draw upon is already baked within you. You just have to peel down more layers, like an onion. Where are you in the peeling of yourself? Remember that you're all the parts of that onion. You may have just forgotten where some of the layers of knowledge and experience are located and how to release them into your life and the lives of others.

It's like the old fable about the blind men looking at the elephant, and they think the elephant is a trunk, or a foot, or a tail, but if they could see more broadly they would see one massive elephant. I think we all do that with our own lives. We kind of focus on the trunk or tail or big ears and don't see the whole picture of ourselves. If you are young and starting out, or even if you're already retired and want to know what else to do with your time, picture yourself looking at that elephant and laughing and saying there is so much more to me than I ever thought.

We all have parts of our life we would just as soon forget about and sometimes it's fine when they stay forgotten. But many times as you're doing some kind of project, you realize *oh my God, is that what I really thought back then?* Which is why when you're older or retired, you might look back on stuff for clues to what you might want to do now, clues that will evoke a brainstorm for manifesting what might interest you now.

Of course it's fine to just be, to not always do. There's a silly phrase that you're a human being, not a human doing. For most of my life I was a human doing who was always striving to achieve something. That's not really necessary. You're probably really fine just the way you are. But I find you have more enjoyment and self-satisfaction if you can be involved in some way with activities that feed a purpose. Adopting pursuits that give you a sense that you're making a difference in other people's lives gives us both the will and thrill to live longer and with more enjoyment.

There is so much need by so many people. Don't you love it when you read on Facebook or in the newspaper about some nine-year-old kid who raised a lot of money to send clothes to a disaster area or some such charitable cause? There are so many opportunities to help other people. I have found, as a theme for me, the more I give, the more joy there is in it. Joy is in the giving much more than in the receiving. When you make a dinner for somebody and they love it, doesn't that give you a lot of pleasure? You have more pleasure eating it too. In creating joy in other people, you're creating more joy in yourself.

One of the big joys for me in getting older is continuing to discover new things about myself. You don't really realize how you might feel about something until it's put in front of you. An opportunity could present itself and the way you react to it tells you something about yourself. Are you going to let somebody know they didn't charge you enough for something you purchased? Are you going to try to take something that's not yours, or are you going to help somebody, even if it's just holding the door for the person coming behind you? Simple acts of kindness and thoughtfulness add up over time to shape the better nature of the human being you most want to be. It is easy to smile more and it seems to create a glow inside too.

If young people don't have real manners today, it's because someone didn't show them. They just haven't had the experience or the awareness to know and they need role models, which is where you and I come in. If they have been taught manners and still don't exhibit any, well that's different.

Practice Keeping Yourself Motivated

If you are like a lot of people, there are times when you are at work and just feel zapped. You can't even describe or explain how tired you are, yet, if you switch it up and do something else for even a short period you can revitalize yourself. Get up out of your chair and dance around, or if that is a totally absurd suggestion for your work environment, take a short walk around the office and see what things you can notice that you never saw before. Taking a few deep breaths always helps me in any situation.

If you can do a different activity and feel that you can put your heart into it, you will definitely be energized. Boredom and repetition kill energy, so it is up to us to find some distraction that will enable us to feel a modicum of peace or happiness. We will likely energize ourselves enough to go back to the task, perhaps with refreshed eyes or mind.

You can even try my approach. I always thought about choosing what color to wear everyday based on the feeling I wanted to express. Red for energy, green for healing, blue for calming, yellow for power, purple for spiritual, brown for grounding, orange for creativity. What vibe are you wanting to send out?

Know that you are the one in charge of YOU and your environment. As restricted as it may appear, it can be modified and changed. People may or may not notice, but who cares! It is all about how you are relating to your environment.

Do what you can to give yourself a boost and try to put a smile on your face. Take the courageous step, whatever that looks like, or feels like, or whatever it means to you.

ℐOIE-ISM #39

*"Anything or anyone that does not
bring you alive IS TOO SMALL FOR YOU,"
is a quote from the poet David Whyte that
I often find myself referring to.* This quote has become
such a part of who I am that it *feels* like a Joie-ism.

ℐOIE-ISM #40

*Sometimes the value of something isn't obvious
and you may not realize it for a long time.*
But if you shift your thinking, everything can look and feel different.
You have to be open to go with the flow because
anything you fight tends to fight you back.

ЈOIE-ISM #41

My biggest learning has been that each of us in charge of our life.
If it's to be, it's up to each of us. We're each more
unique than a snowflake. Be Your Own Elvis!
(Elvis Presley was a one of a kind and so are you!)
If you don't know Elvis, please look him up!
Like all of us, he was quite an original.

CHAPTER TEN

Be Open to an Unexpected Awakening

JOIE-ISM #42

Be open and curious so joy has a way
to find you when you least expect it.
Ideas can be accepted slowly and thoughtfully,
but give new concepts a chance to make an impression on you.

Like so many other big shifts in my life, my unexpected spiritual awakening happened quite by chance. I guess the Universe was ready for me to discover the inner bliss and joy of experiencing a new consciousness. Many refer to this uplifting state as awakening to awareness of the Christ Consciousness, which refers to the Christ Light within. This is not about organized religion, but rather about the inner light and knowingness that glows from your soul and expands through your whole being and shines in a big smile on your face.

Spirituality was a word I would never have used during the first half of my life. I just didn't give it any thought, but I was aware of, and paid attention to intuition and an inner knowingness and guidance. I suspected there must be some force or energy that gives you those "aha" moments and insightful quickenings about people and events. I could sense the energy of other people and sometimes knew instinctively who to gravitate towards and away from. I probably would have referred to all of that in those days as gut feelings.

Religion had been something that seemed didactic to me. It was there, it was stuff you would be taught in Sunday school, but nothing I really related to. Once I was told in Sunday school that God was up in heaven (to me, that translated to an old guy with a kindly face and a long white beard, likely sitting on a cloud), my first airline flight had proven to me that there was no one up there fitting that description. I just thought about religion as something like algebra—you were supposed to learn it, but I wasn't aware of or hadn't experienced any personal connection to what I had been taught about it.

One symptom of my awakening came after my husband Lew and I had been in Hong Kong where Lew was meeting with clients and I was meeting with Sesame Chicken (my most favorite food in Hong Kong) and having the fun of making custom business suits. As the end of our fabulous trip neared, I realized that it would be a good idea to head to a spa before going home because the awesome Hong Kong food had resulted in me gaining a pound a day and I was having concerns about fitting into my clothes.

Since the next stop for Lew was in Orange County, California, I thought I could find a spa with a diet program and hang out while Lew worked. While I tried closer places, they could not accommodate me, and I almost seemed to be guided to Palm Springs, a place unknown to me. After several tries to go to other spas, I ended up booking at a place called The Palms of Palm Springs, which had a diet program.

Being fancy at the time, Lew arranged for me to go from Orange County to Palm Springs in a limo. I was dressed like a business woman and arrived expecting a large, elegant hotel of some kind. Instead, I was greeted by a scruffy spindly-legged man in khaki shorts and a taut white T-shirt barely covering his huge belly. He had a toothpick stuck in the middle of his mouth, and grumbled at me that I better hurry or I would miss lunch.

Once on the grounds, I realized it was a quaint, if not somewhat drab facility that looked a bit like a Girl Scout camp. I was shooed to the dining room to be greeted by someone who said they would bring my lunch. No menu. No choices. This already felt all too rustic for fancy me.

A lovely woman named Elinor came to join me as I was the only person in the dining room, and explained that they serve one entrée each day and that I could request tuna or egg salad if I notify them by 11 a.m. She mentioned a 4 p.m. yoga class which delighted me, but said I would need to bring my own leotard and a robe if I expected to shower. Very strange to me, as I expected a full-service hotel.

I had arrived with luggage that would have contained something for a White House dinner and almost any occasion, but alas, no leotard! Their gift shop had exactly one leotard, a shiny red thing, and I was thrilled to have something. I checked into my room and ran to yoga, having changed into the neon red leotard. I really enjoyed the experience of the yoga class.

By dinner, I called Lew and told him, "This isn't for me. It's too rustic. Please send the car for me in the morning. They have a morning walk at 7 a.m. and I might as well do that, so please have me picked up around 9:30 a.m."

That was the plan, but spirit had other ideas—big ones.

When I returned to my room, I was looking for a pillow and found it on the shelf in the closet. When I reached for it a strand of rose quartz beads fell into my hand. I have always loved crystals and stones, but didn't know much about rose quartz at the time; I later learned that they represent love and many serene, caring qualities. I asked if anyone had forgotten them, and the office people just shrugged and told me to keep them. Those beads became a symbol of how my consciousness shifted and those beads are still adorning a statue of Quan Yin that sits on my altar in my home office. I have had them near me for decades, and somehow every time I glance at them I am reminded of the great shift and beginning of my spiritual journey that started on that unexpected trip to Palm Springs.

It seemed really easy to wake up early and get to the porch where everyone was meeting for the 7 a.m. walk. We stretched and chatted and soon I was off walking, first on the street and soon after on a nearby dirt path. I found that looking at the mountains, the alpenglow of rose and lavender caressing the tops of the mountains, and the sunshine bathing the day in newness and light, created a deep sense of peace, a feeling that was very unfamiliar to me.

You're home said a small voice deep within me. I was enthralled by the experience, and really didn't know what to make of it. I loved the sense of freedom provided by the big sky, the glowing mountains, and the knowledge that in being there I was just fine with nothing to do, no one to call, no deadline to brood about. I was just being and not doing.

The hour walk seemed to condense into minutes, and soon we were back at The Palms for breakfast. Most of the guests found tables together inside the dining room. I opted to take my tiny muffin (the consistency of a hockey puck) and a small slice of cantaloupe outside to one of the patio tables. I wanted to face the mountains and just drink in their energy. After breakfast I found myself calling Lew and surprisingly, I heard myself say, "I'm not coming back, maybe ever!"

I had never experienced a feeling quite like that before. Doing nothing besides taking walks, yoga, exercise class and eating well-prepared healthy food was pretty cool. My life had always been full of busyness and expectations and doing things and making lists, yet in that place of magic in Palm Springs I was able to experience a new way of being. Life there was just at a much slower pace with no demands on my time, and I loved it. Of course, I was on vacation; but somehow that energy shift meant more to me than I could have imagined, and I was definitely up for staying far longer than I originally planned.

So, I stayed at the spa and lost a pound every day following their healthy lifestyle. The best realization was that at 2 p.m. California time my office back in Florida was closed. Yes, the presses were running and would be until 11 p.m., but I was free to not think about business at all—totally rare for me, and since we had been in Hong Kong earlier, I was now away from my business for as long as I had ever been.

Two women I met at the spa suggested that I read a book they had just finished called *Jonathan Livingston Seagull* by Richard

Bach. The book was fairly new and was acclaimed as a "book for spiritual awakening." Timing continued to be perfect, as the three of us had many long conversations and walks together.

After a week, Lew was ready to go back to Florida but I was hesitant to leave Palm Springs. We compromised and checked into the Sheraton Palm Springs and stayed another week. Finally, Lew HAD to get back to Florida but I went back to The Palms for yet another week. Ultimately, when I went home I often found myself longing to return to the serenity of Palm Springs.

One Sunday, Tony and I were the only ones in the pressroom. He was running a job that we were under deadline to get out, and I was helping with the bindery. I looked out the window and commented to him that I wished I was in Palm Springs. I will never forget his words: "You own this place. You can be anywhere you want."

Though it isn't really that simple, the intriguing idea remained with me. If you own a business you are responsible for your employees, the payroll, the clients and all that. I could not imagine just going back on another vacation. As it turned out, I did go back several times a year; catching the red-eye after work and being driven from Los Angeles to Palm Springs by the same wonderful driver, Bill. I also always requested room 7, and never stayed anywhere else.

I did that for years, and it only made me want to be there more. The first time I ever heard New Age type music was there on my first trip. I had booked a massage, and this new artist Steven Halpern had just recorded an album. I have loved Halpern ever since as he introduced me musically to the kind of bliss I found there. Years later, I met Steven at a sound healing conference, and he was delighted to hear about the role his music had played in my life.

I kept reading spiritual books and soon found that I was gravitating towards meditation, crystals, stones, and lots of the New Age stuff. The effects of meditation, holding wonderful crystals or wearing them as pendants, just felt the same as a big exhale, calming and focusing me with a sense of peace and release that felt really good. I found myself not only drawn to this stuff, but for the first time didn't feel a need to sell it to someone else. I might mention it, and people were always commenting on my stones and crystals, but I would do little more than say thank you to them. Very different than when I would want to share everything and felt some need to convince someone to love it also. My new interests were so personal, I didn't feel the need for approval or anyone else having to get enjoyment from them.

At Christmas one year, Anthony, another Tony, an experienced printer and wonderful man who ultimately ended up managing our night shift and did so many other important things for the company, gifted me with a large desktop amethyst crystal that brought me to tears. "How did you know I would like that?" I asked. He nodded with a knowing smile: "I just did." That crystal sits fairly close to Quan Yin and the rose quartz beads on my altar, and has also always been close to me.

I never thought of myself as spiritual even at that time, and remember being chagrined and perplexed by a local psychic people had raved about, who told me I was very spiritual. I thought she was really off-base, but as the years passed, I surprised myself with the realization that she had been right. My many visits to Palm Springs definitely were times of spiritual growth and enhanced awareness. Something definitely blossomed and was uncovered there.

Palm Springs continued to be the epicenter of my spiritual growth and really was a big change from my former life as a businesswoman. I recall going to a wonderful yoga conference that featured a live presentation by singer Deva Premal. Her music still is what I play every day, especially just before going to sleep. She and her partner Miten have created some of my favorite music, and in recent years they sometimes add Manose to their tour. He was also a frequent musician at the Center for Spiritual Awakening in Pacific Grove, California when I attended there.

When I first heard Deva in the early 1990s, I also met several new friends who were interested not only Hindu chants like Deva sang, but also in the philosophy itself. One said she was a

Hindu, when actually she was a Jewish girl from Studio City in Los Angeles! It didn't make sense to me at first, but I was curious and took their advice and went to hear Gurumayi, the present-day guru of Siddha Yoga.

Entering the room to see Gurumayi felt like a complete shift in energy and vibration. She was seated on a stage, cross-legged, wearing a peach-colored draped robe. The energy in the room was palpable and overwhelming. When she smiled, it was as if a radiance projected from her to each individual; possibly thousands of people were in attendance. She was truly awesome and inspiring and spoke so distinctly, with humor and joy and wisdom, straight from her heart. I was transfixed by her presence and her charm.

Her talk was memorable, yet I don't recall anything specific that she said; just that it was like no other event I had ever attended. The quiet was intense when she would pause. Her every movement could cause sighs, laughter and immeasurable delight. No one clapped. We seemed to know not to break the spirit and energy of the room. I left there intrigued and wanted to study more about Siddha Yoga.

My girlfriends and I would meet and discuss books and the fundamentals of Siddha Yoga, and when I moved to the Carmel area, I found a regular meeting of people who were also interested. Many new friends and I had a connection with Siddha Yoga, and a surprising number also went to the Pacific Coast Church, which is now the Center for Spiritual Awakening in Pacific Grove. The minister, Dr. Bill Little, was also very knowledgeable in Eastern traditions and able to combine diverse interests perfectly in his presentations.

I took several online courses from Self-Realization Fellowship founded by Paramahansa Yogananda, in Encinitas California, and still receive their mail and remain loosely a part of their community. Yogananda is credited with bringing yoga and similar studies to the West. When you visit the meditation gardens in Encinitas, you cannot help but feel a unique peace as you sit watching the pools of koi fish. It was as though I had to go from a go go go lifestyle to a stop stop stop one. I found these studies, people and locations so different, yet so wonderful, that to this day it brings a big smile to my face to participate in any of their programs and events.

While still in Florida, I had met Deepak Chopra at a Religious Science Church in Boca Raton. He had recently come to the United States and was affiliated with Maharishi Mahesh Yogi at that time. He spoke about the value of meditation in such a way that it inspired me to ask him for a teacher in the Fort Lauderdale area that Lew and I could meet with. It turned out that the person he recommended formed a class that Lew and I attended. We each received a mantra, and to this day I use it when I begin to meditate each day. I was not halfway about anything. If I liked it, I LOVED IT!

Once back in California I was free to pursue all of these spiritual avenues, learning about these different yoga sects. And starting to hike had to be about as life-changing as anything. The hiking club really was the nexus for my greatest friends, and two that I did not mention in the context of hiking actually will fit perfectly here. Both Michael and Gene were past presidents of the hiking club and the three of us would spend many hours talking about spirituality, the life history of Jesus and Mary Magdalene, and their family travels to France. Once, when Lew and I visited Aix-de-Provence, I wanted very much to find the famous cave there where Mary Magdalene had been, but it was not some place you could hop into a cab and ask to visit. I think if I had been there with Michael and Gene we would have found it.

Once I moved to Carmel Valley in Monterey County, Michael and Gene would visit and we continued our talks as we watched the moon rise on Carmel Beach. Michael was the best instigator for great ideas to go to the beach, and bring my dog Yogi, who seemed to fit right in with our little group. We also visited at Michael's cabin in Mountain Center, California, and called ourselves the "Ulurus," after the famous Ayers Rock in Australia. Michael had Australian roots and Uluru represented freedom, which we were feeling after careers in the business world. Those talks with them were key to my continuing study of spiritual books and related philosophies.

I cannot encourage you enough to find people with whom you share common interests. As with anything else, to ripen friendships takes time and shared experiences. Being out in nature, walking or hiking, is an ideal way to connect with others and deepen your bonds with them.

Carmel Valley is its own special paradise. We lived up a hill that was across from Garland Ranch Regional Park, a sprawling reserve of over 4,000 acres of hiking trails, mini lakes and parkland. That was the major attraction in our choosing to live there.

Shortly after moving, I went on a guided hike led by a man who would become a dear friend and hiking buddy, Larry. His enthusiasm for hiking was like mine, and I was delighted to hear that he also was a docent at Point Lobos State Natural Reserve. He suggested that I would be a great docent, so I went and took the training and Point Lobos became the next center of my universe.

It is considered by many to be the crown jewel of California's state parks. As I was joining this program, I had no idea that the timing would be particularly appealing, as I had mentioned that I had been in publishing and graphics. Their longtime editor of a docent newsletter was really tired of doing it, and nobody else wanted the job. Seemed I was wooed and beguiled to "puhleeeze" take on the task of getting out the newsletter. He had been doing a few typewritten pages and had some black and white photography included. Since I had been used to producing wow! materials at JMG, I thought of it as an opportunity to finally be a graphic designer myself.

I purchased Microsoft Publisher, which seemed easiest to learn, as the programs that my graphic designers had used were really for professionals—I figured since I had less than a month to get out the first issue, I better learn software made for anyone. I was thrilled to learn how to create headlines and already knew the most important thing was to format the publication so that items could just be dropped into specific categories each month. All of us docents were recognized by the green jackets we wore when on duty, so I came up with "Green Jacket Happenings" to report on various small items of interest to our group, as well as on those for several other ongoing sections.

I always had a theme, color photography by some of the greatest nature photographers, as well as skilled docent photographers. Being able to work with a printer was an old thrill that I missed, and I did the actual binding and mailing myself, or with helpers from the docent ranks. Loving art and design, I tried to make each issue better than the last one. Many people commented and complimented me, and they especially loved that I would find postage stamps that matched the theme of the issue.

It was a great volunteer job for me and I loved it. I did it for about five years until we began to travel for periods longer than a month, which meant I would be gone for longer than the entire time it took to get out an issue. The joy of having been a part of the docent organization cannot be understated. I loved explaining the mating habits of marine mammals (Did you know only the female harbor seal routinely chooses her next partner and isn't the greatest mom as she teaches her pups to swim and how to find food, but is gone in an average of five weeks!) Otter moms, on the other hand, will keep their pups for up to ten months. Since otters mate by the male holding onto the nose of the female and bloodying it, it is no wonder that they are in no hurry to leave their pups!

The stories were delightful to tell, and I especially liked to take school groups and explain to kids some of the wonders of the natural world. I was careful to do it with humor and have them really enjoy themselves. I recall several groups of kids that lived in the Salinas area, which was about 30 minutes away, who had never seen the ocean before. I could not believe that! A natural resource so nearby, they marveled at seeing the waves and large body of water.

The joy of nature is something everyone should experience to the degree that they can become excited about it. As docents we would walk the trails answering questions from visitors or working at specific places where we could explain the artifacts and information key to our natural history, shorebirds, plants and geology. What I learned was that I never got tired of learning. People who volunteer time in this way are a special group and many of them, like me, loved to hike and teach the joys of what Point Lobos had to offer. I still go there whenever I can get to that area and it remains one of my favorite, most wonderful experiences and places to be. I keep my green jacket in my car to this day as I visit state parks often, and would volunteer again if such an opportunity arose.

When living in Mill Valley, I also served for a short time as a volunteer at Muir Woods. The history and majesty of those redwood trees are one of the most enthralling sights against which to put our humanness into perspective. Breathing in the exquisite energy there is a one of a kind magical nature experience anyone can enjoy. Not surprising, both of these parks attract several hundred thousand visitors from all over the world every year. If you have not had this experience, I encourage you to treat yourself. If you find yourself near a state or national park, be adventurous and check it out.

Discovering the Joys of Sound Healing

Ever have a birthday gift open up a whole new world? My daughter Debbie gifted me with a large quartz crystal bowl that had a beautiful sound in the tone of A, and we played it together and fell in love with the sounds that would vibrate and be generated from its magical tone. Debbie had a masseuse friend who played a bowl like this at the beginning and ending of a massage.

My next bowl was gifted to me by my sister Karen and brother-in-law Freddie. I played them both before I would meditate. Crystal quartz bowls introduced me to sound healing in a more personal way, and I have been engaged with it ever since.

While still living in the Palm Springs area, I would attend workshops and events occasionally held at the Center for Spiritual Living Palm Desert (my original church) that sometimes included these bowls or an element of sound. I loved participating in drumming circles, and the chanting that was part of Siddha Yoga.

I learned of a new organization in San Francisco called Globe Institute of Sound Healing, now called the Sound Healing Center, and this was about the time that the first pioneers in the field were doing their work. Ironic, since using sound for healing goes back millennia to the drumming and chanting of ancient native tribes. I met David Gibson, founder of the Sound Healing Center, who continues to sponsor sound healing conferences every year in San Francisco. An especially important one occurred in 2008, where almost everyone involved in sound healing seemed to be in attendance.

Studies were being conducted on the effects of sounds on patients in hospitals and new books seemed to be published about this topic with greater frequency. A whole new world of vibration and sound and its effects on human consciousness was being studied. At this huge gathering I met people who I remain in touch with. Many international musicians that comprise the New Age and toning sounds genres were represented by their music or in person.

My eyes became as big as saucers when I first saw a display of crystal singing bowls that were made of gemstones. Beverly of Crystal Tones at Mount Shasta, California took the time to explain the various tones and how they worked together and how they were made. I was enthralled and left that conference having purchased a sound healing chair complete with headphones and glasses with flashing lights to transport me to other levels of consciousness, almost like climbing into a rocket ship. Soon I was studying with people who have now become the masters of this field.

Tom Kenyon was someone I later learned about and went to his teaching events. He still does some events and you can find him online to learn more. Once I moved to Carmel Valley, I met one of my favorite teachers, Randy Masters, and I still try to get to his various workshops whenever I can get to the Santa Cruz area. Once you attend these conferences you meet so many people with similar interests and they lead you to others. This kind of networking is valuable for learning more and meeting new contacts in any field that interests you. There are always events, and today the internet makes it much easier to find what you are interested in.

In honor of a special birthday, I really wanted to visit Beverly at Crystal Tones in Mount Shasta, and perhaps treat myself to a bowl. I made plans with Debbie, who was living in Chico, to drive to Mount Shasta for a specific appointment with Beverly. At the last minute Debbie was unable to go, so I tried calling Jay, a young man there who had once driven me back to Carmel Valley. Jay was available and once again, me not enjoying driving anywhere by myself created magic. We had so much fun before my appointment looking in many shops and experiencing Mount Shasta.

Finally, I went to see Beverly and it seemed that time went by in a flash. She and I were so into her teaching me about the bowls that we agreed I would just stay and we would play. Soon Jay was knocking at the door. He was excited to show me something he had found at another store that was about to close. We rushed over there as he was wide-eyed about a flute, which I got and we both ran back to Beverly. What happened was magical. Beverly and I played the crystal bowls and Jay played the flute I had gifted him, and a concert, known also as a soundbath, of beautiful sounds was created. It was almost midnight when we finished. I could have stayed for more hours. One of the most special experiences ever!

My home has a special sound healing area and tarot table set up in a dining area we didn't use and it brings me great joy. The co-founders of Crystal Tones (CrystalTones.com), Lupito and Paul, are mentors. Every time I see Lupito I learn more about playing the bowls and am enthralled to share soundbaths with friends.

Does this give you any ideas for what you might really like to feature in underused areas in your home? It's really delicious when you discover something that resonates with you, and all of these surprise elements that bring you joy can open new worlds of experience in your life.

Accelerating My Spiritual Growth

Feeling grounded in the different kind of beauty that was the desert surrounding the greater Palm Springs area seemed to be for me the most fertile area I could have been in for spiritual growth and new awareness of ongoing consciousness raising concepts. One person I met would introduce me to others and the nexus of Paul Heussenstamm introducing me to Brugh Joy ushered in the next great time of my personal spiritual maturation.

W. Brugh Joy, M.D., was an early pioneer in the discovery of energy medicine. He could feel energy rising from his patients, and his colleagues thought he must have lost his mind. He found himself no longer able to practice medicine with his group, and began to embark on the greatest change of his life. His book, *Avalanche*, describes this, and it launched another phase in my life. Brugh gave many talks and workshops that I attended both at Paul's house and at other locations. Brugh's other book, *Joy's Way*, became a part of these discussions too.

One time I went with Brugh and about twenty others on a retreat in the Arizona desert. Brugh was a mystic pioneer who studied the profound mysteries of human consciousness. He taught that we are not really in charge and that we need to get in touch with forces and "patternings" (his word) within ourselves. He would expound on a community of beings within ourselves, and that our dreams are a resource to help us access these other dimensions of ourselves. To Brugh, each of us is a mystery of multilevels of being that we can choose to uncover.

It was while I was with Brugh in Arizona that I witnessed something so incredible that I would not have believed it had I not seen it with my own eyes. The ten days were structured almost like an ecstatic dance experience that builds to a peak, and then slowly descends. It built up slowly and we would listen, have various discussions and learn about books, including some wonderfully insightful children's books. By days four and five we were instructed to fast and drink only liquids. Soon we were in silence, and at that point we were told we would see an actual transfer of energy.

Okay, I thought; *I'm here.* It was almost like the saying, "In for a penny, in for a pound," but I really did not grasp exactly what Brugh was speaking about. It must have been about the seventh evening and we had been fasting for two days when we were ushered into a room that had a black velvet curtain hanging behind a small stage. There was a long table where we were instructed to sit opposite each other. The table too was covered in black velvet. Brugh intoned some chants, spoke some unusual sounds with some strange music playing softly in the background. This probably took from forty minutes to an hour. All was hushed and then he pronounced that we would "see energy." He instructed us to stretch our hands out on the black velvet with our fingers apart and our fingertips about four or five inches from the fingertips of the person opposite us. It felt very comfortable as we had been building up to this moment since we arrived. Without really being aware of how Brugh was building to the crescendo of this moment, I soon saw thin white plumes of energy extend from my fingertips to the person opposite me; and saw the same thin wisps of energy emitting from that person connecting to the energy from my fingertips.

Talk about being stunned! I had been hearing about energy medicine, energy transfer, energy this and energy that, but yikes, this was so amazing as to be astonishing. Had I not seen those little plumes that looked like very thin smoke, I would have simply thought it was something that you might feel, but not actually see. It would have been incredulous.

Brugh was determined that he could make us see energy if he created the conditions to make it happen, and yes he did. It was at this same Arizona retreat that we learned about Voyager Tarot, as Brugh had a special way of using those cards as a tool for both intuition and insights for the people in attendance. We were sitting on the floor in a long oval-shaped circle and he had each of us read the card that the person next to us had picked. When it came to me, he spoke to the group longer than he had about anyone else's reading of a card, and said, "Joie, you have a special gift for this." With a big grin on his face he added, "You should hang out a shingle and call yourself Madame Zora."

I did readings the rest of our stay there, and read for many of the other attendees. The concepts and ideas flowed as a combination of intuition and picking up energy cues from the person I was doing the reading for. I have continued to do that. The creator of that Voyager Tarot deck is James Wanless, Ph.D., and he and I became friends. I took many of his classes and became a Certified Voyager Tarot Reader. I still use the deck for my readings that Brugh gifted me in Arizona.

James also has written many books and combined spiritual and business aspects in some of them. When I lived in Carmel Valley, we lived within minutes of each other. I continued to do more workshops with both Brugh and James and found it quite surprising that they had never met each other, although each would refer to the other's work in their workshops.

For many years, Lew and I joined with others for a New Year's celebration (which also is our anniversary) at Asilomar, the special resort in Monterey County that hosts business and metaphysical conferences, including the annual Science of Mind conference. Brugh would usher in each new year there with a special music and dance event that included a ceremony, sharing his wisdom, and always unique gifts for all the attendees. He would also choose a Voyager Tarot card for the year (there is a specific formula for which card matches a particular year) and do a reading as part of the opening ceremony.

One year I suggested to Brugh that he consider having this reading done by the creator of Voyager Tarot, James Wanless. Brugh was delighted by this idea and it was a joy for me to introduce them to each other at Asilomar. James' forecast became a part of the following conferences that Brugh did there, and it was a metaphysical win-win for them and so many of their followers.

Deepening the Spiritual Journey

In 1988, a dear friend of mine, Bobbe, was headed to the Pritikin Longevity Center in Los Angeles, and I wanted to surprise her and show up too. Pritikin was about health, and they assigned you to a doctor. I was running JMG Publishing at that time, and was shocked when my assigned doctor said to me, "You keep this up (meaning the constant selling, deadlines and appointments) and you will drop dead." Though I didn't really believe that, he did get my attention. He asked me if I had heard of Louise Hay. I said, "I don't think so." Across the street were the offices of Louise Hay. This doctor was quite insistent that I go over there, so I went expecting a little cottage of some kind, but it was in a typical office building. I bought some of her tapes and her most famous book, *You Can Heal Your Life.*

Once I finished all of the mystery thriller books I could find at Pritikin, I picked up Louise Hay's book and stayed up reading it until 4 a.m. My pulse was racing and I felt I had picked up something totally life-changing. I was so intrigued by hearing her say "This is Louise Hay" at the start of each tape, that I came to feel a closeness to her. What I found particularly inspiring was the idea that your thoughts create your life. What you think about, you bring about. She was all about forgiveness and accepting people as they were because how you felt about anyone or anything was really entirely up to you. Forgiveness did not mean condoning, it meant an acceptance of someone else so that YOU could experience an opening and a freedom in your own thinking about them. Don't give your power away. Other people do not create how you feel about living your life.

None of this was as simple as flipping a switch for me, but I did feel very good listening to her speak. She had a voice like honey, slowly pouring wisdom, and the cadence was peaceful and lulled me into a naturally relaxed state about stuff that probably had bothered me my entire life. You can create the life you want, she taught me, and you can heal past hurts and experiences. How? Change your thinking and that will change your life. I was pretty good at creating my business life and my life with friends and my husband, but my emotions could go all over the place and I had never had a roadmap of any kind to follow to bring them to a centering peace.

Later in 1988, I had the thought to go and meet Louise. I called her office. She wasn't available but I left my number and said I would very much like to speak with her. A few days later, using the speakerphone, I answered a call and heard, "This is Louise Hay" exactly how she sounded on the tapes!

"Really! Is this the real Louise?"

"Yes, it is!"

I asked to take her to lunch and she suggested the following Wednesday. I don't know if she recognized the area code or if she didn't dial the call herself, but I agreed to meet her. I went from Florida to Los Angeles just like that! I brought with me a layout of a newsletter that one of our graphic designers, Chris, did for her, and it was perfect. She loved it! She had talked about living in "The Present Moment" and so that is what we named the newsletter.

She called in a newly hired guy, Reid, and while he liked it, he thought that they didn't have the financial wherewithal at that time to produce it. Now those of us familiar with Hay House know how momentous a moment this turned out to be. Reid Tracy came to be the president and CEO of Hay House and has done more than any individual to bring spirit and business and books together. He is a marvelous, brilliant man and created Hay House as we know it today.

I hugged Louise and was able to share with her what a difference she had made in my life. I considered the trip a great success. Years later, little parts of the newsletter we put together would appear here and there, such as our "Dear Louise" letters. I still have a copy of that original newsletter layout. Maybe someday if I meet Reid again, I can show it to him and we can laugh about it.

That Pritikin trip in 1988 was the catalyst for me wanting to sell JMG Publishing. I recall going home and asking my accountant to find me a buyer. He did, but I was so enthusiastic about Pritikin that the buyer wanted to go too. That delayed the sale. He had intended to purchase it for his son-in-law who worked in the printing business. During the meeting it was obvious to me that he was thinking he was doing a good thing, but he actually was attempting to control his daughter and son-in-law's life. That never works and the couple separated before he could buy my company.

It wasn't until November 1989 that my company was sold, and after that I needed to sell our office building. Once that all happened, California and Palm Springs beckoned. My favorite place in the desert at that time was called Rancho Las Palmas, as JMG ironically had done the brochure for that property and all of us had loved it. The photographs of the homes and grounds were very enticing to me. I looked there with the idea of purchasing a condo and met a realtor named Bobbie. After spending some time together and looking at properties, Bobbie thought I would love a church that she knew about. It turned out to be the original church of what today is the Center for Spiritual Living Palm Desert.

All of these centers eventually dropped the word "church," and the founder of this organization, Ernest Holmes, whose Founders Church was in Los Angeles, liked to think of the them as institutes, or places of spiritual learning. Today they exist all over the world as various Centers for Spiritual Living. For me, this turned out to be a very big deal. The first time I attended, Bobbie dropped me off for the 8 a.m. service. I loved it. "Wow, people here think like me!" so I stayed for the 9:30 a.m. service. Continuing to be enthralled by what I heard, I remained for the 11 a.m. service. Afterwards I asked. "How I can join?" After selling JMG Publishing and the office building in Fort Lauderdale, a place in Rancho Mirage we called a vacation home was purchased. I have always referred to it as "my magic house," and I began to take the classes at the center.

My enthusiasm grew with my discovery that I had truly found a spiritual home. I never felt that I fit anywhere in terms of a religion or connection to a higher power. I felt a certain emptiness about not quite connecting to something larger or more meaningful in my life.

The teachings from the book *Science of Mind* filled that void perfectly when I first was introduced to it. I loved the minister,

Dr. Tom Costa, who was my primary teacher, and a well known figure in the *Science of Mind* world. I ultimately became, after several years of study and an oral exam, what is known as a Practitioner. I became licensed to do special prayer treatments and appear in the services. I don't know if it would have been possible to integrate this newfound peace with a business open 16 hours a day that had daily deadlines, but it would have certainly been a valuable and helpful method for me in coping with daily stress and unpredictable situations. I did not discover *Science of Mind* and its teachings until six months after JMG Publishing was sold. Interesting timing.

At the time I joined it was called Religious Science. I loved the concept of things having a basis in natural order and science. If you plant a tulip you don't get a daffodil. If you believe a certain way, the results will be there for you. I realized that what Louise Hay spoke about were actually principles of Religious Science. When I first became involved there were two separate organizations based on *Science of Mind*; one was known as Religious Science International, which was the umbrella organization of my *Palm Desert Church of Religious Science*, and the other was called *United Church of Religious Science*. Eventually they merged, and the name was later changed to the present-day *Centers for Spiritual Living*. The principles have not changed.

Music as the Language of the Soul

One language that everyone relates to in some way is the language of the soul . . . music. In high school my friends and I would sometimes go into New York and hear Dizzy Gillespie and other jazz greats on 52nd Street. The wild thing about growing up in New York is that we didn't realize at the time how blessed we were to be in close proximity to true greatness.

The music I heard in the city was the standard bearer for what I thought of as great music. There were so many genres. I heard really great musicians without ever realizing that they were some of the most accomplished who would turn out to be all-time greats. When I lived in Greenwich Village while I was finishing college at NYU, my friends and I would often go to the Village Gate to hear some of this great music.

As I grew spiritually, all sorts of new music got added to the mix. My interest in *Science of Mind* also influenced my new tastes in music. The Center for Spiritual Awakening I attended when we lived in Carmel Valley on the Monterey Peninsula, was very much influenced by our minister, Dr. Bill Little. He loved to incorporate Hindu philosophy and I found myself studying Siddha Yoga and enjoying music that related to it. One of my favorites today is Snatam Kaur. Musicians I learn about or hear at soundhealing conferences become new favorites almost as quickly as I discover them.

Had you told me when I was working at JMG Publishing that I would one day be listening to this stuff, I no doubt would have rolled my eyes. Why am I telling you this? Because as we live and grow it is fine to be attracted to stuff, or to try stuff, that would never have made sense before. Why limit our taste and expressions of delight in music or art or anything? Sometimes I was surprised that this New Age sound, which was really music that had been around for thousands of years, reached us in the West.

Everyone starts someplace, and being someplace at the time you choose to go there can teach you something, or make you aware of some new concept that changes your life.

Prayer as an Agent of Change

As I took the various classes and read Ernest Holmes' books and other books related to *Science of Mind*, I took a greater interest in doing their form of prayer that is known as a Prayer Treatment. It consists of several steps and the prayer addresses each step to form the treatment. Several years of study precede learning how to do Prayer Treatments, as that is key to becoming a Practitioner. I find Prayer Treatments to be effective and comforting and don't recall ever doing one either for myself or anyone else that did not bring a sense of peace and relief.

I truly believe that the prayers change the outcome of situations, although there is no attachment to the outcome when you do a prayer for yourself or anyone else. It is about trusting that your highest good manifests and that in itself is an awesome turning over of power to a more divine source than yourself and the machinations of your mind. I think we all can benefit from incorporating beliefs like these, as they are about finding your autonomy and freedom. This has been a natural fit for my way of thinking.

When you want to be with like-minded people who share your beliefs, then you have found your spiritual community and it is truly a joy. You will never feel alone, or without a way to help yourself through whatever challenges that life presents. It's all about trusting a higher power, and consciously putting yourself and your life issues into a relationship with a much larger perspective. Embrace your power and follow your own path and inner guidance. Trust that you know what job to have, where to live, and whom to associate with.

No one knows you better than you, and if you realize that everything you need is already within you, you will prosper. Literally find it within yourself to create what you want. It is truly important to trust your own intuition, and if you are not sure, meditate on it, swing a pendulum, or find a method of connecting to Source (Spirit) that clicks for you. There are limitless choices but they all can reinforce the power you have within yourself to heal and create your desired life.

You CAN Do It!

JOIE-ISM #43

Anything new needs to be nurtured.
The seed is planted but if you just mindlessly crush it
under your feet you will not know of the joyful growth
that seed can add to your life. It could be increased
love, peace, joy, creativity, spirituality or a feeling like a wonderful
exhale. Give yourself a chance to experience new feelings and ideas
and see where they blossom within you, and in your life.

JOIE-ISM #44

Find situations where you are with like-minded people.
It feels delicious to be with people who have shared interests
and think like you. In doing that it gives you a chance to blossom.
When you share your thoughts with people who think like you,
they affirm what you are saying and that makes you feel
good because it's like a first step in discovering the bigger picture.
There is probably something in everybody you could relate to.
It could be a philosophy your share, or an approach to spirituality,
or fun interests. Have your interests narrowed with age?
You learn about yourself through others. If a book is recommended
to you, check it out. *Trust that the Universe will send you messages.*
The more you are in tune with what's presented to you,
the more conscious and aware you are.

JOIE-ISM #45

Many of us initially reject ideas that become our favorites
and continue to resonate with us, because we have
deepened our connection to our inner selves. There is so much
that we cannot fathom, but we must begin someplace
on our unique journey of inner wisdom and self-discovery.
A book, a painting, a piece of music, anything can trigger
a whole new world for you, if you are open and receptive
to considering new thoughts and ideas about your life.

About the Author

An entrepreneur from the age of eight, Joie Goodkin's first business was renting comic books to her friends. She later founded, on her kitchen table, a countywide magazine in Florida, that she eventually sold as part of a Wall Street underwriting. She also created a printing, graphic design and publishing company recognized nationally for its unique service and willingness to try anything to meet a deadline.

Joie's career and civic contributions have been honored with at least 50 awards for her community service and business accomplishment. She also did a stint fighting crime with Crime Stoppers, a national organization that she helped bring to South Florida.

She won multiple sales and marketing awards, including one she co-won with Wayne Huizenga, founder of Waste Management, AutoNation and Blockbuster Video, given by the South Florida Sales and Marketing Association. She was named Woman of the Year in Marketing and Communications from the South Florida Advertising Federation, was a recipient of the Florida Region Silver Medallion Brotherhood Award from the National Conference of Christians and Jews and of the Golden Rule Award from J.C. Penney. She is listed in many Who's Who type publications.

An avid hiker, she loves being in nature, creating art, listening to an eclectic mix of music, and reads like "a vacuum cleaner." She lives in Northern California with her husband Lewis Goodkin, and at present, no dog.

Acknowledgments

For all the people who helped me along the way, especially my husband Lew, and my friends Kate and Lisa, thank you.

Gratitude to Nancy. This book would not have materialized without you.

And Randall, thank you for your wisdom and insights on the best way to tell my story.

Made in the USA
Lexington, KY
22 November 2019